Unicorns Adult Coloring Book Vol 4

60 Entertaining Stress Relieving Unicorn Patterns

By Omar Johnson

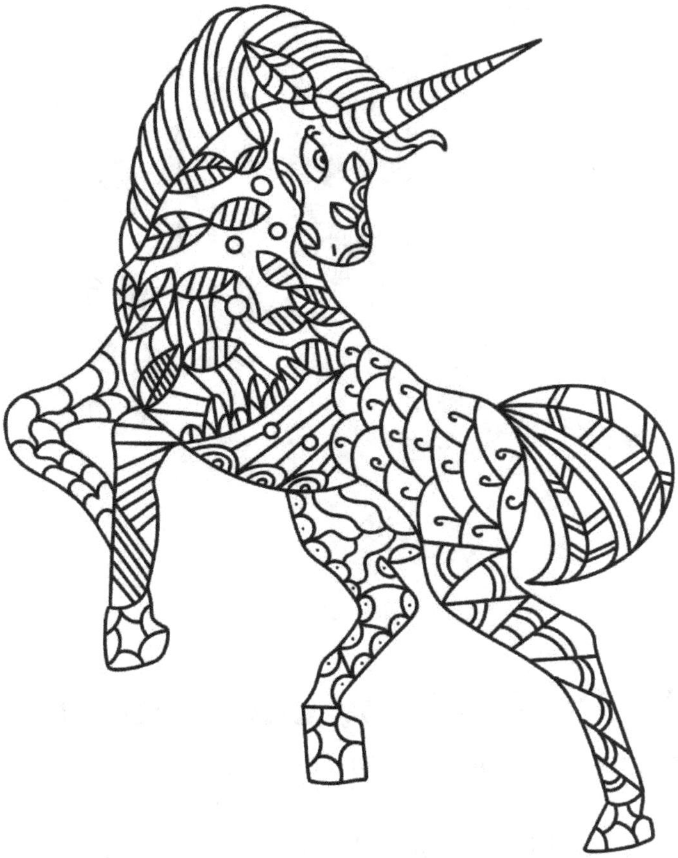

Get Your Free Butterfly Mandala Coloring Book

Visit

HTTPS://WWW.ADULTCOLORINGBOOKSFORYOU.COM

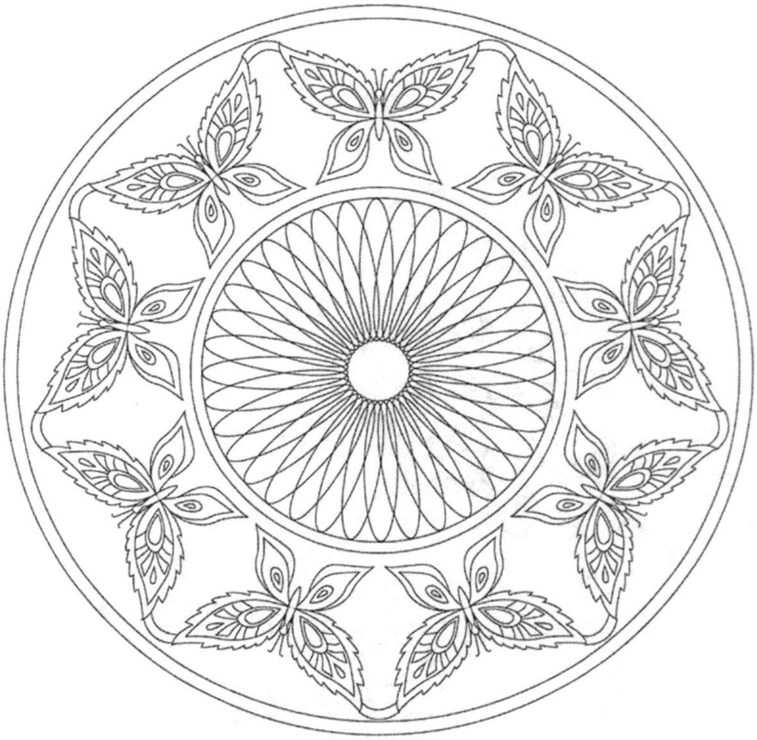

Make Profits Easy LLC Publishing
omarjohnson@adultcoloringbooksforyou.com

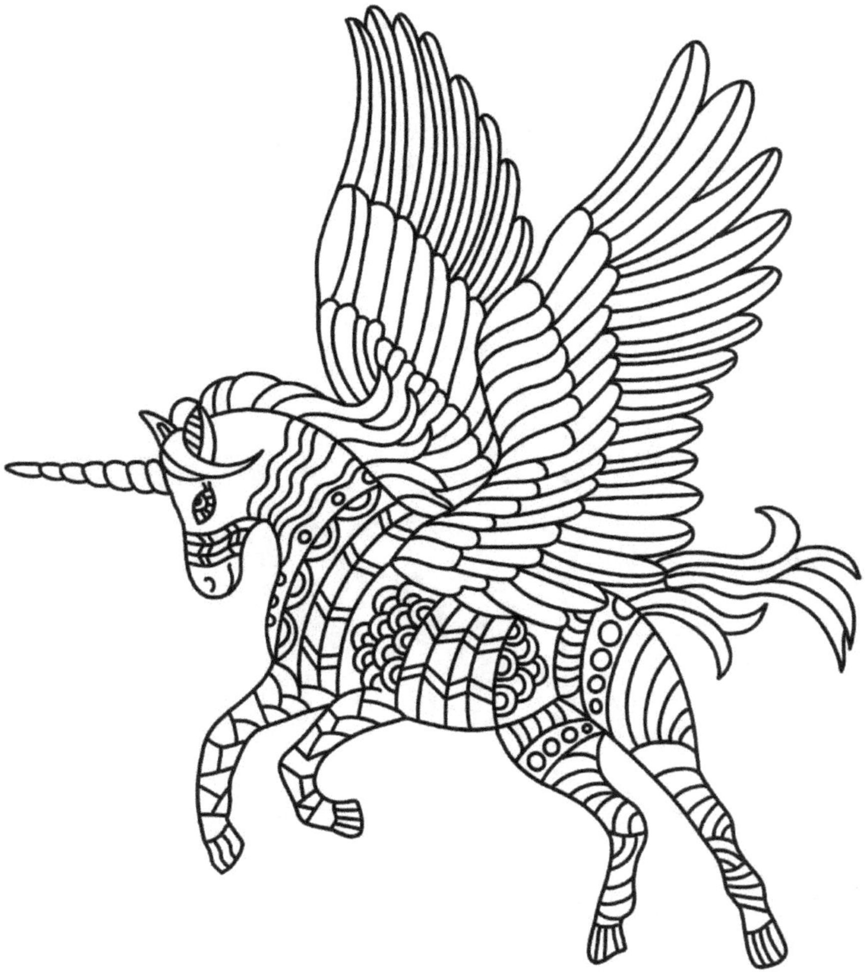

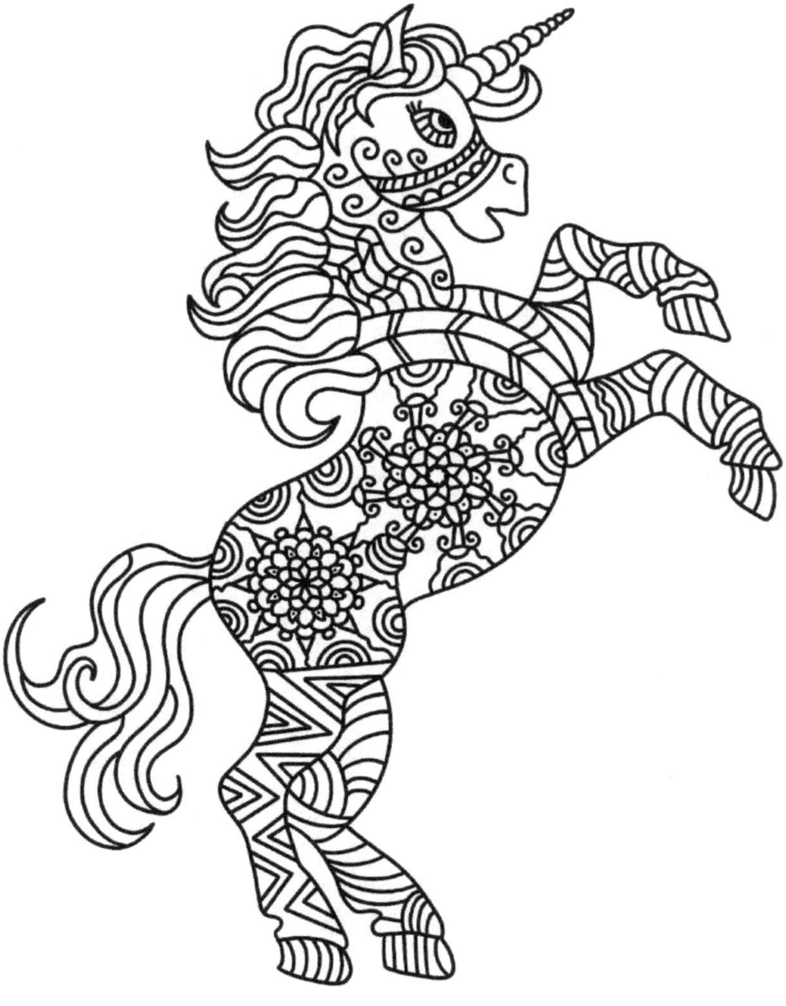

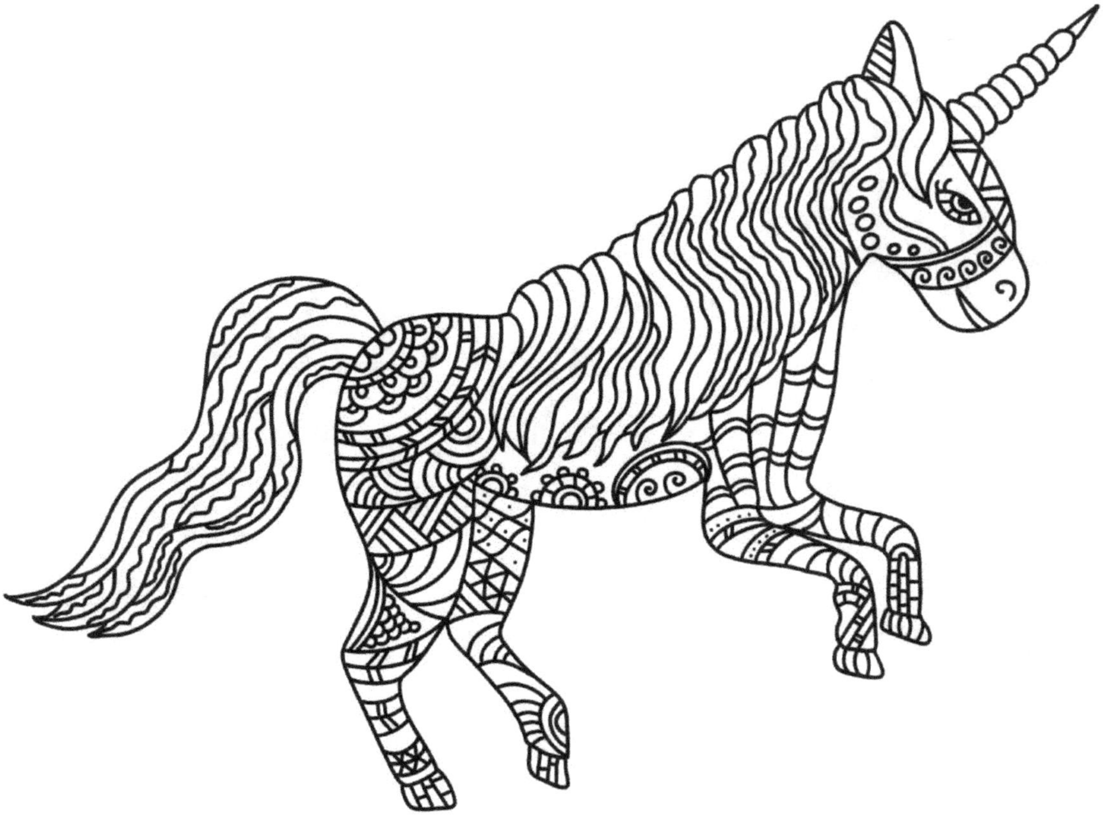

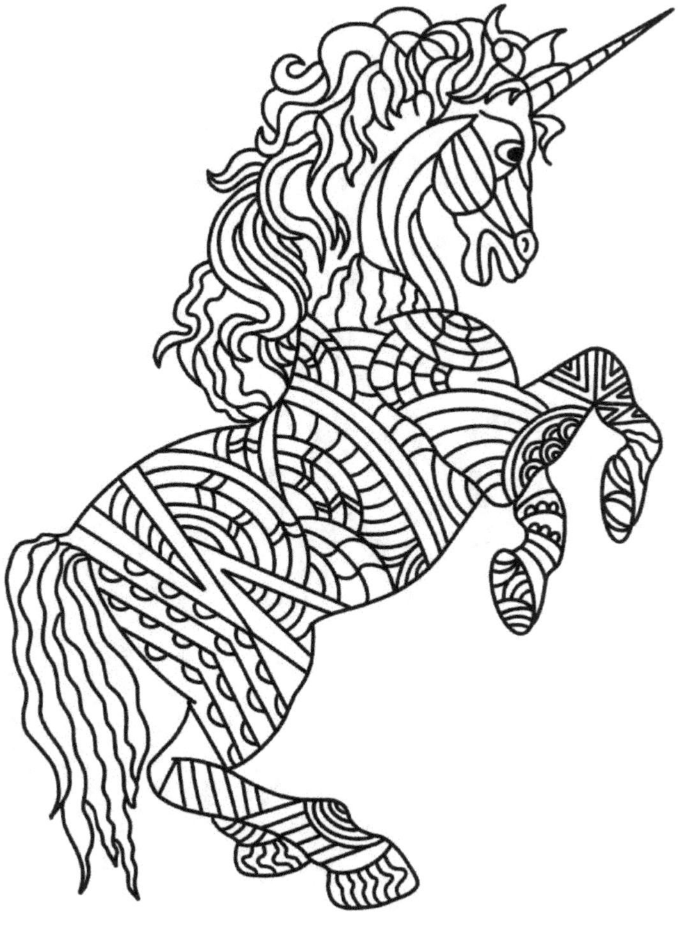

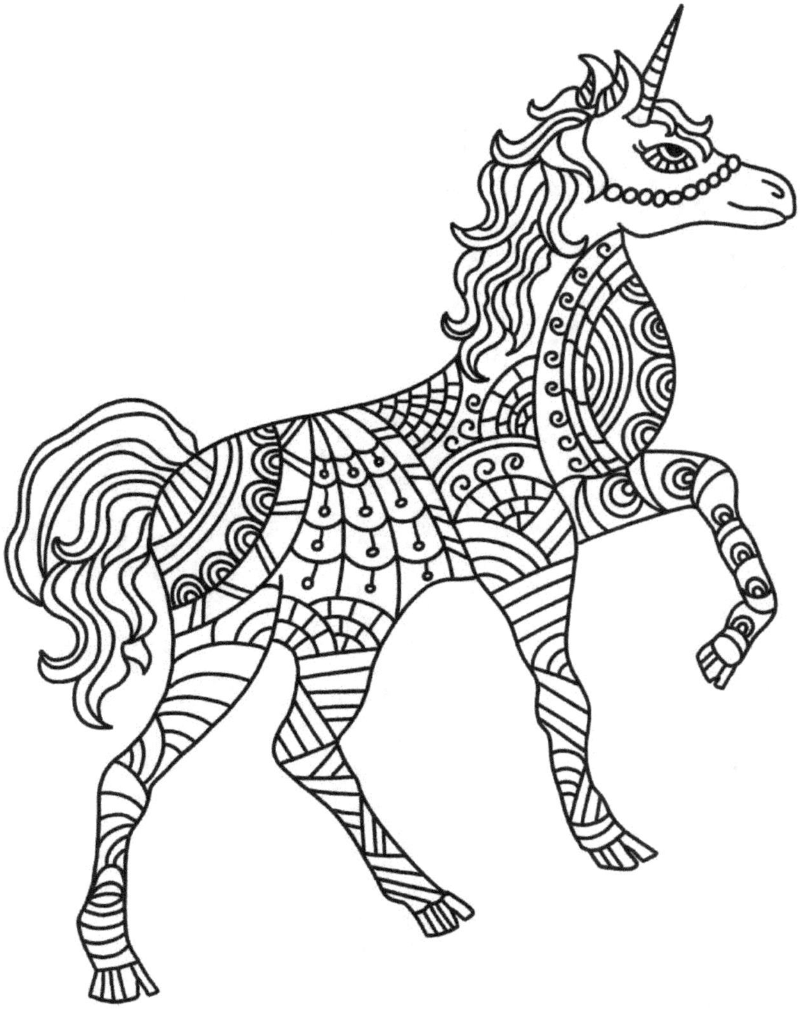

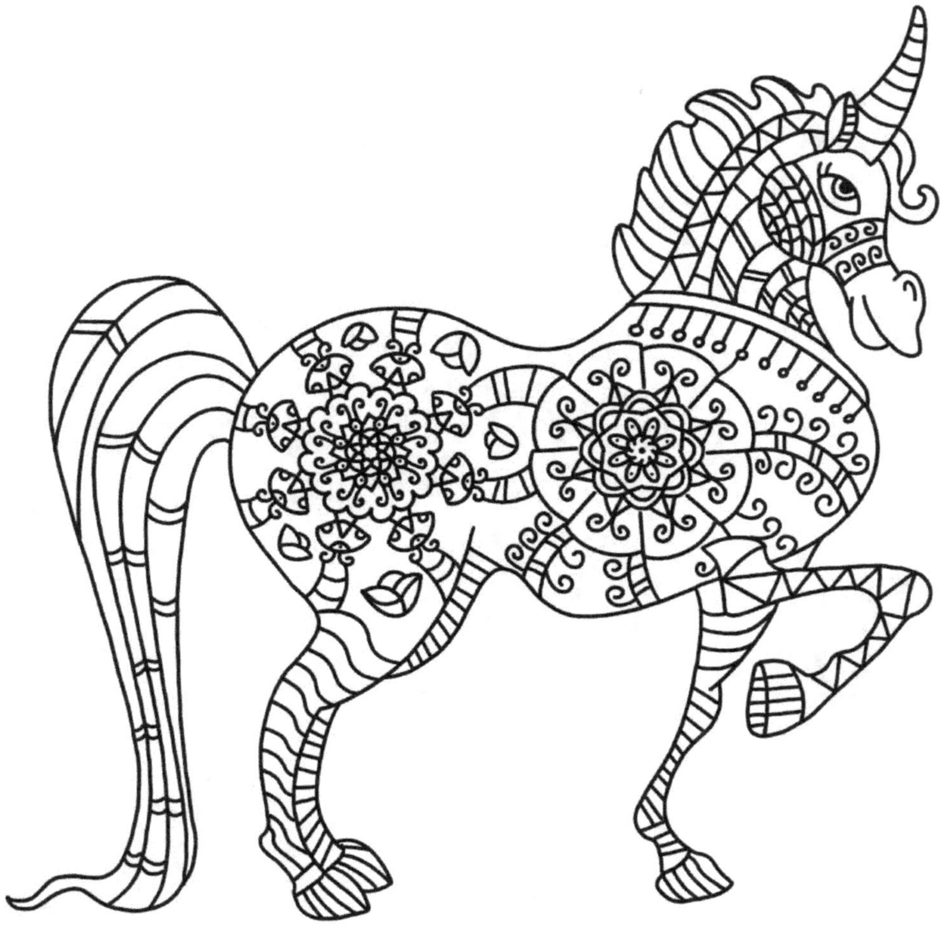

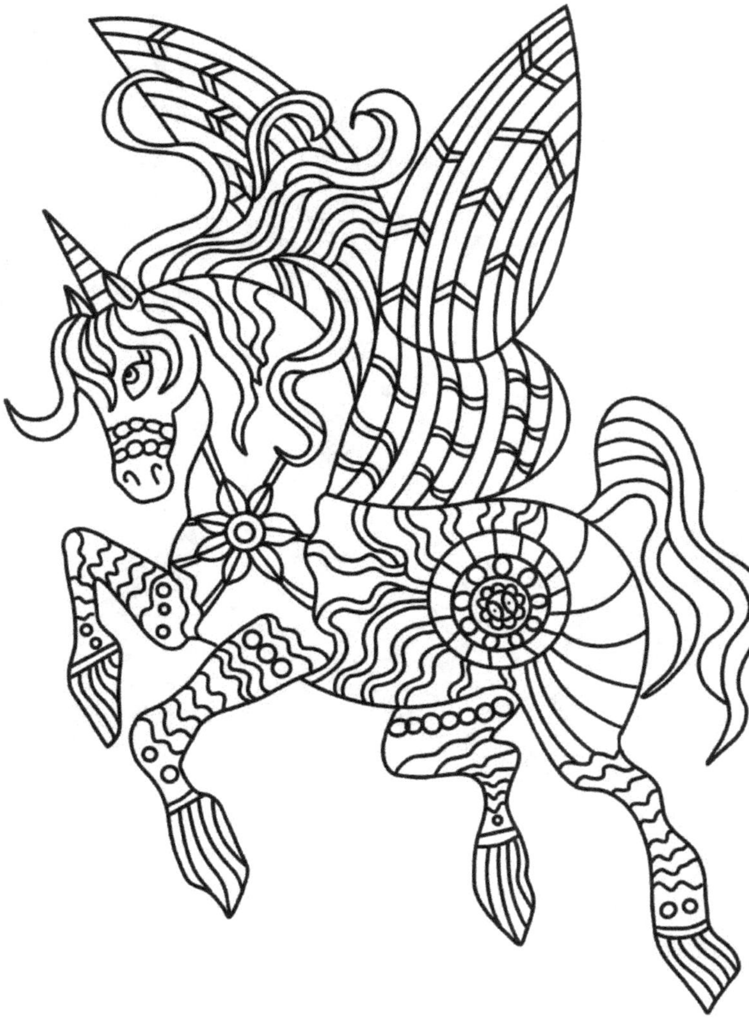

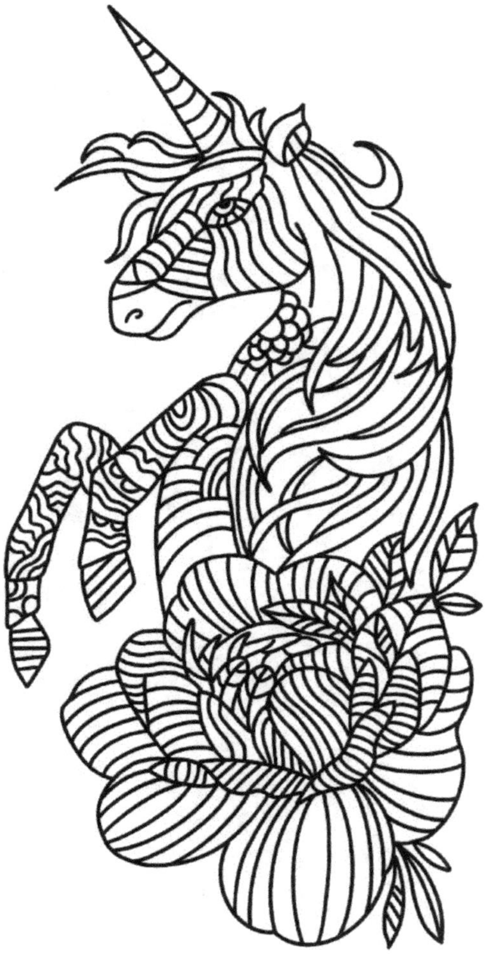

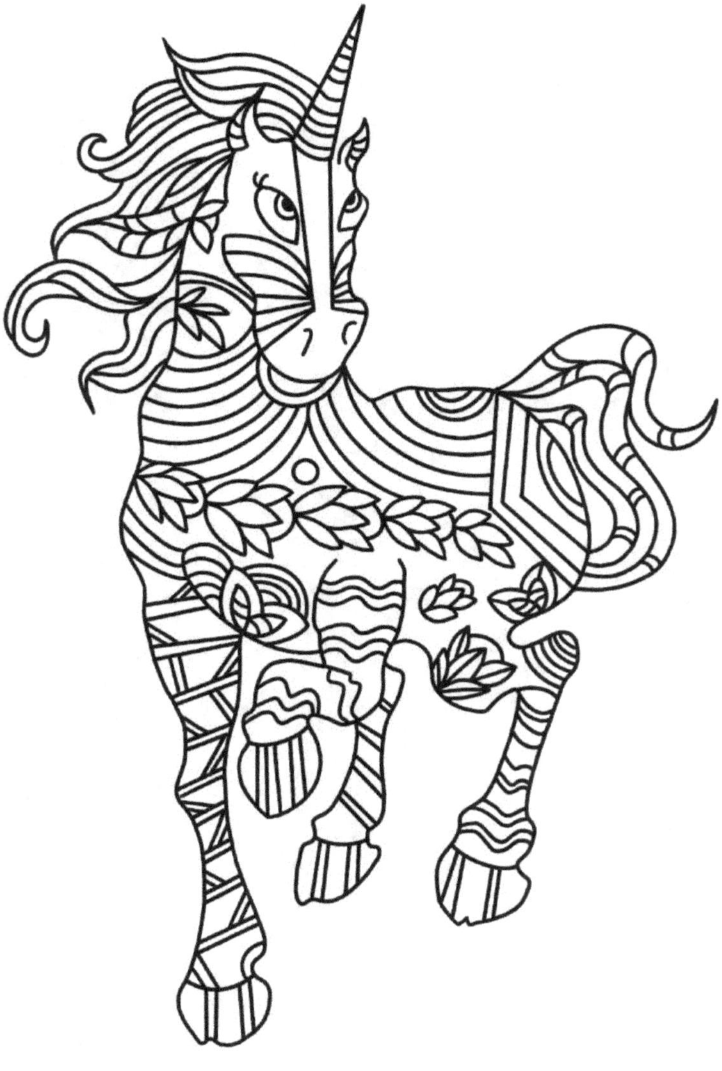

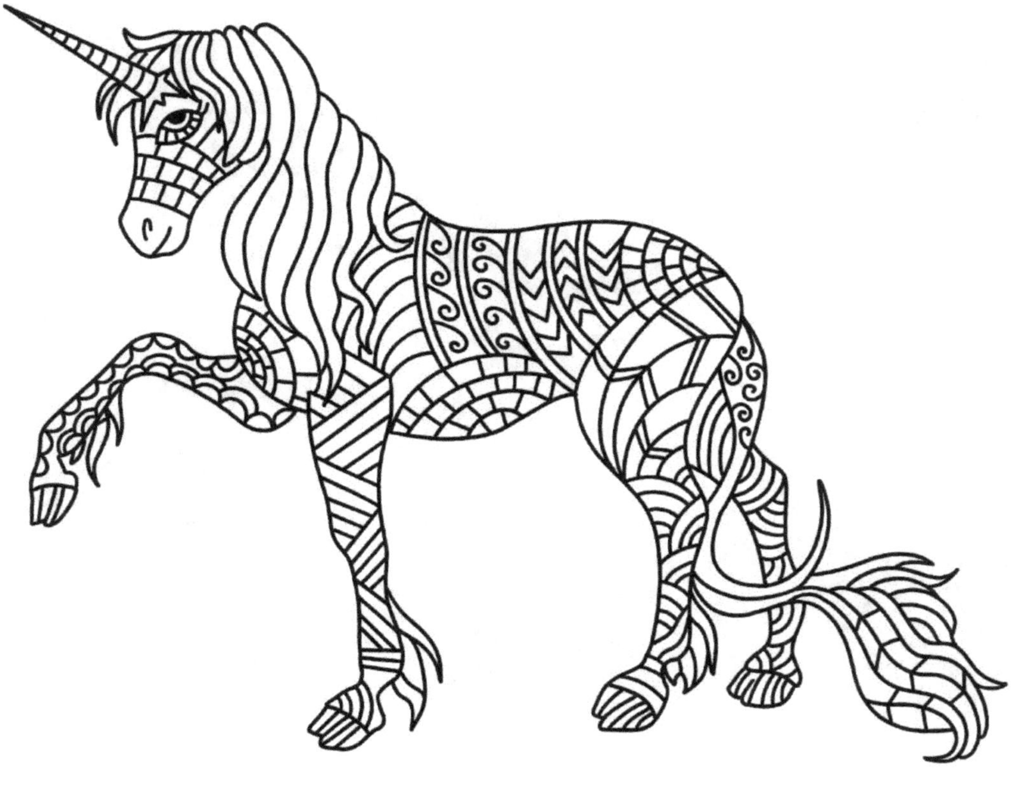

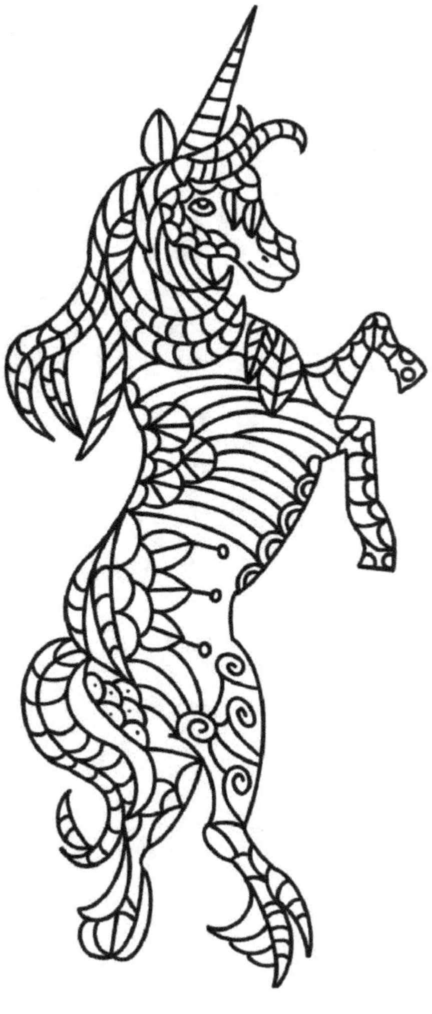

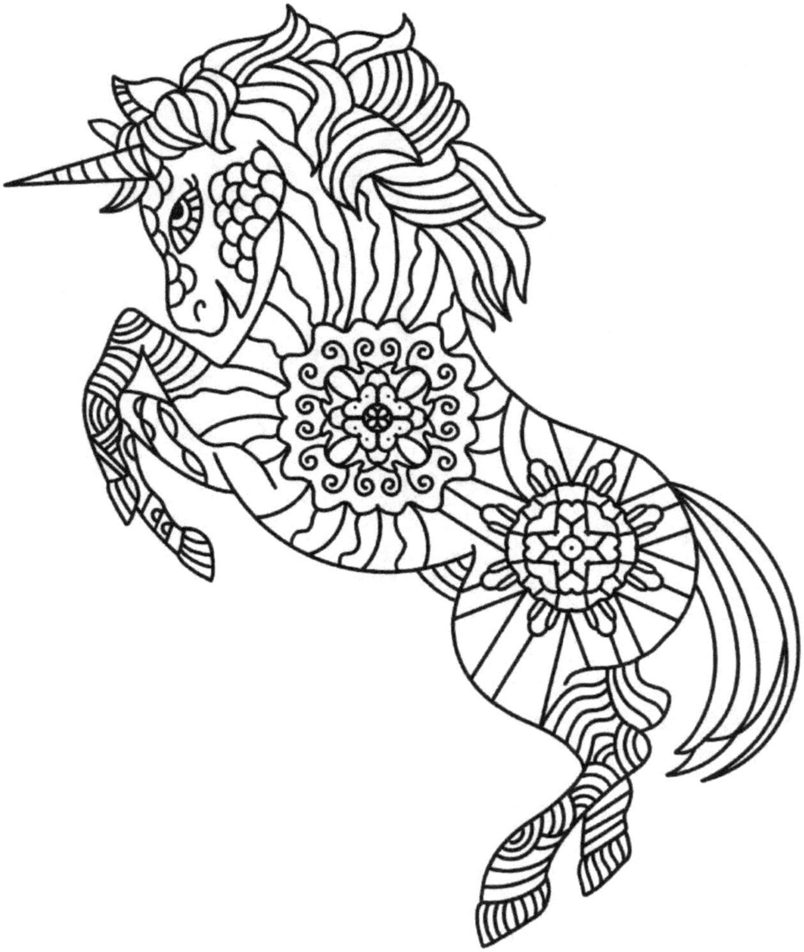

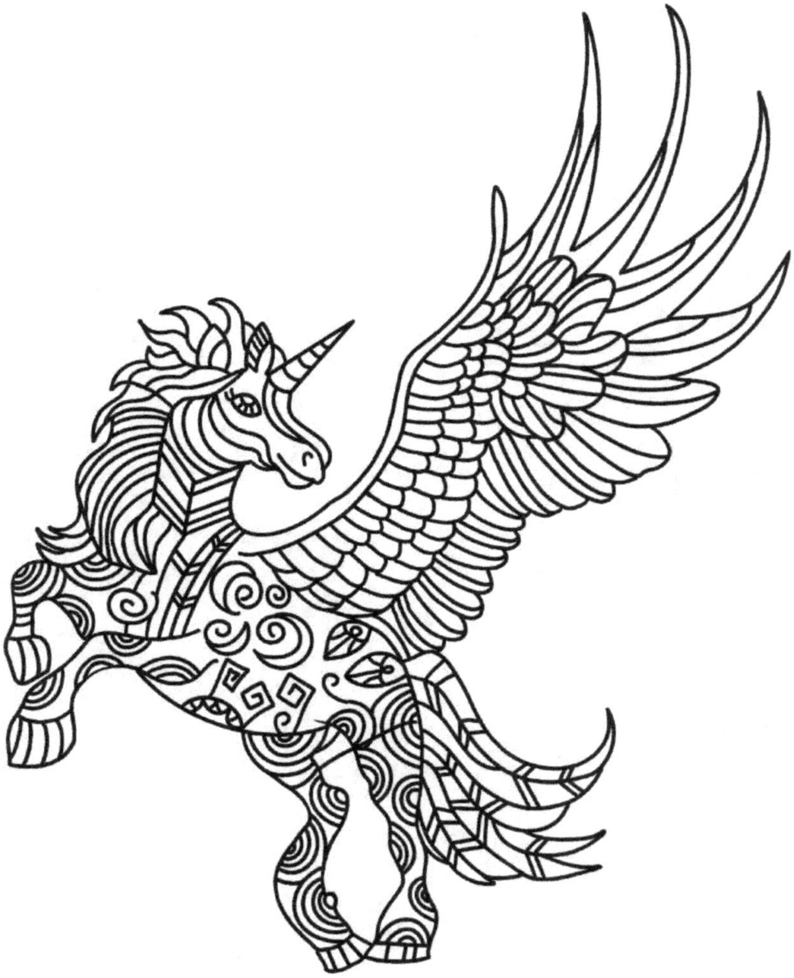

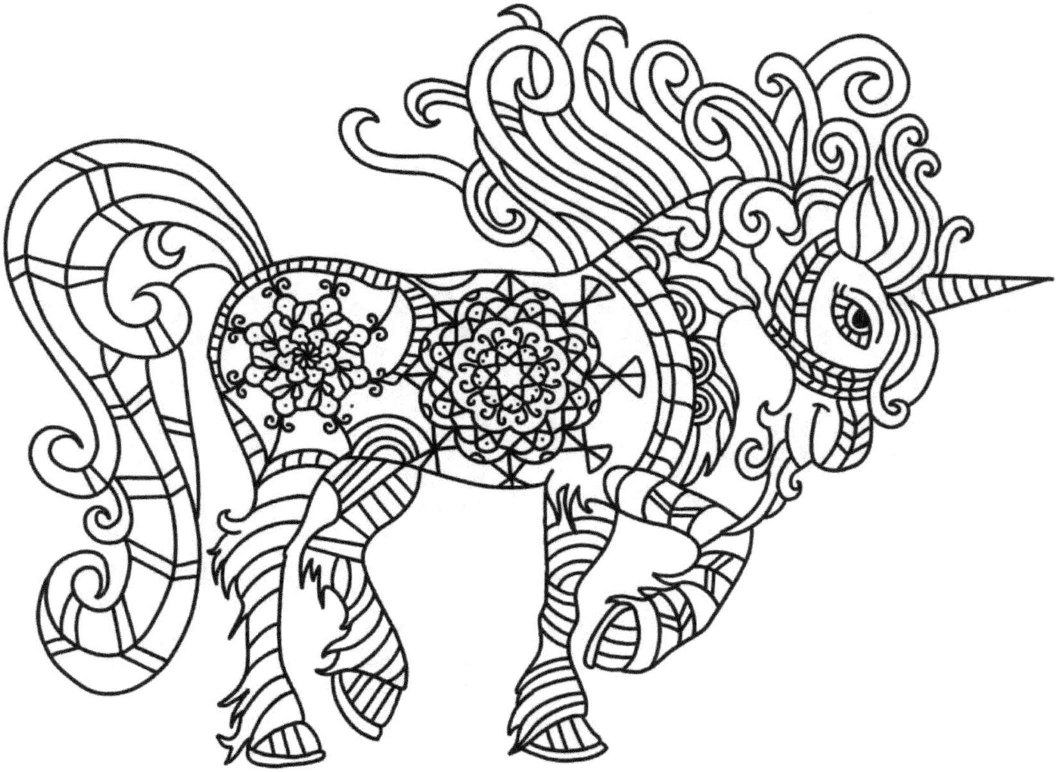

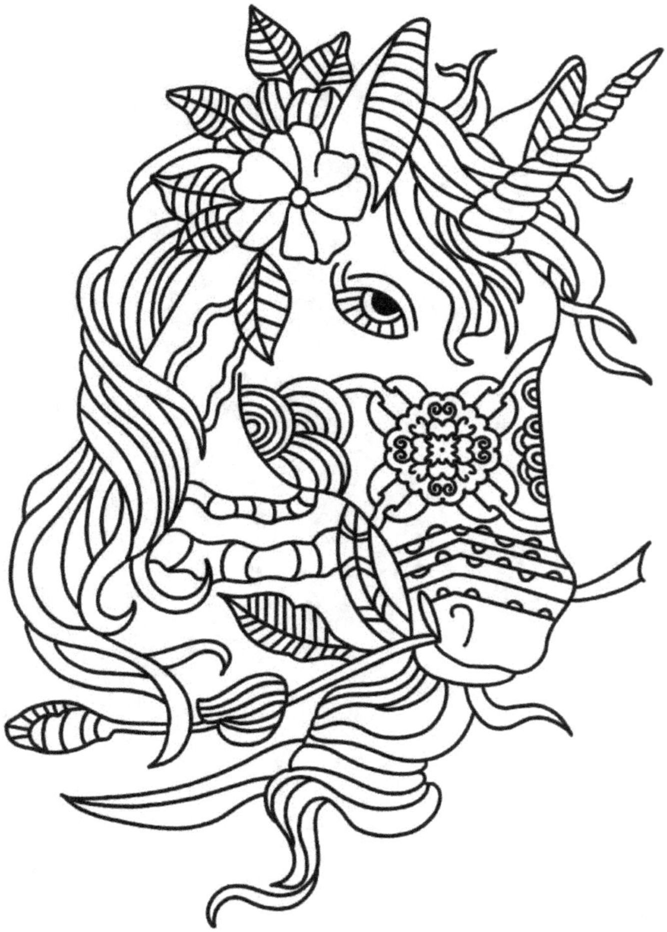

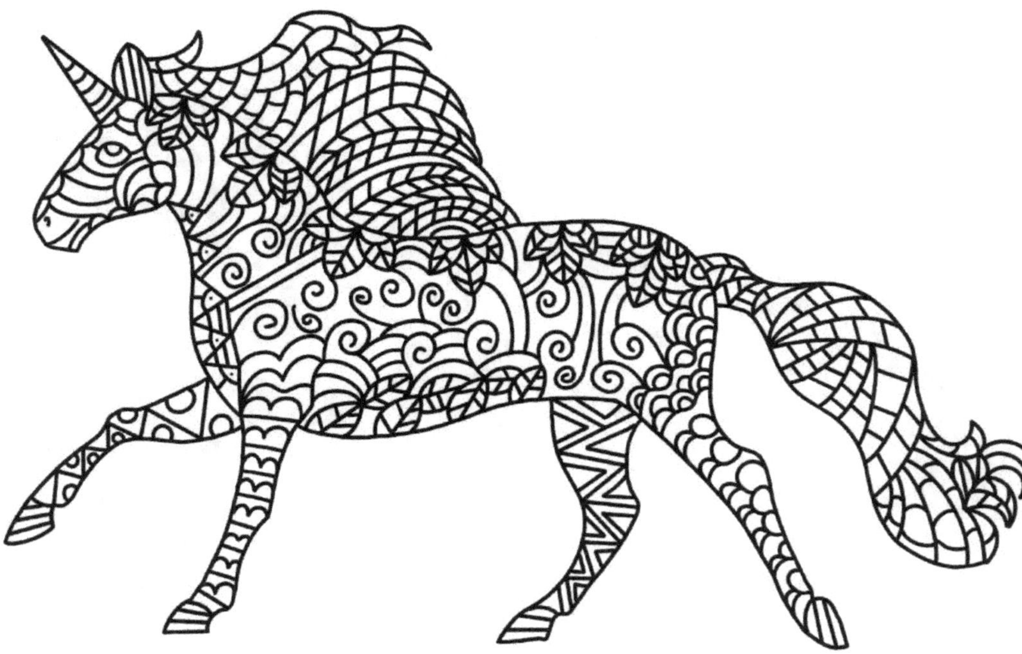

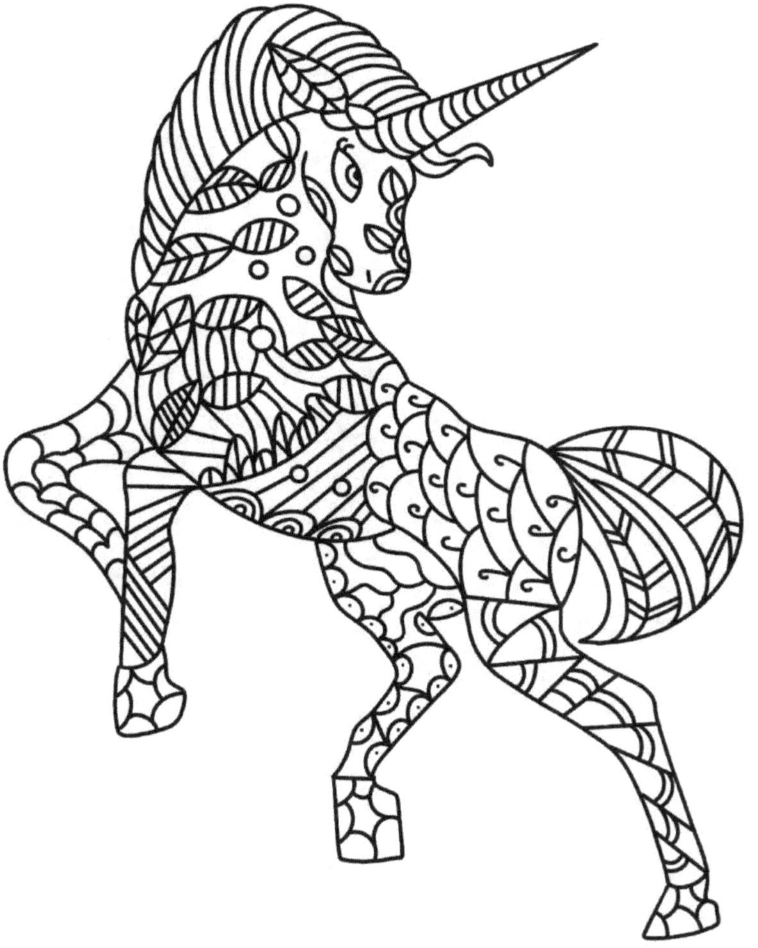

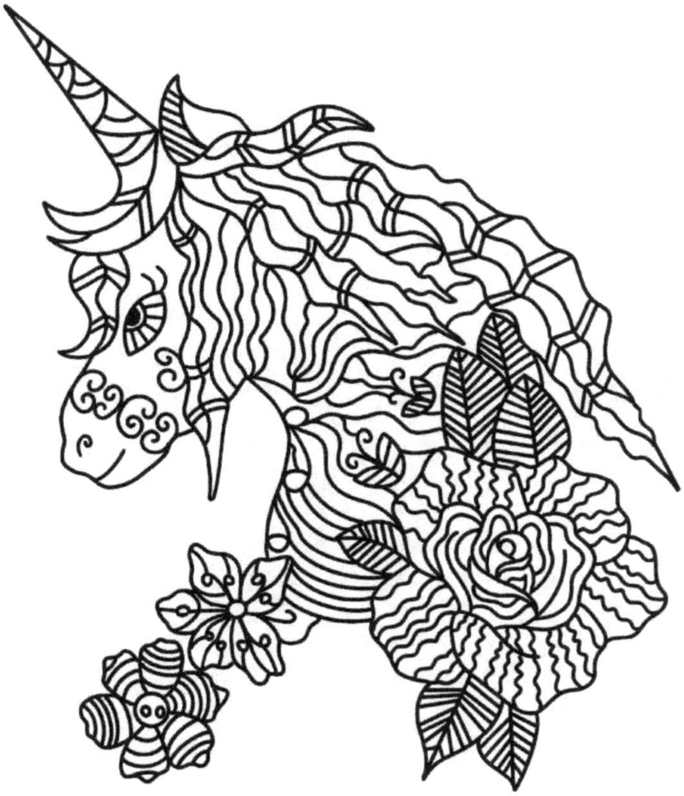

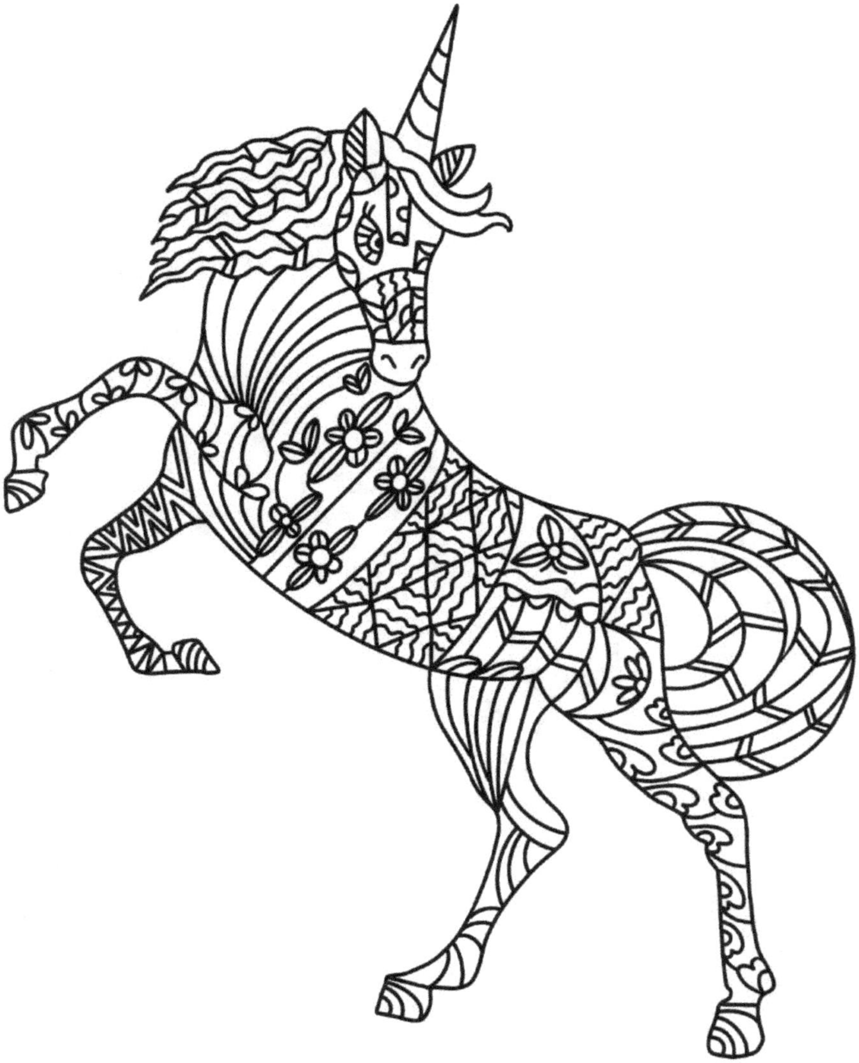

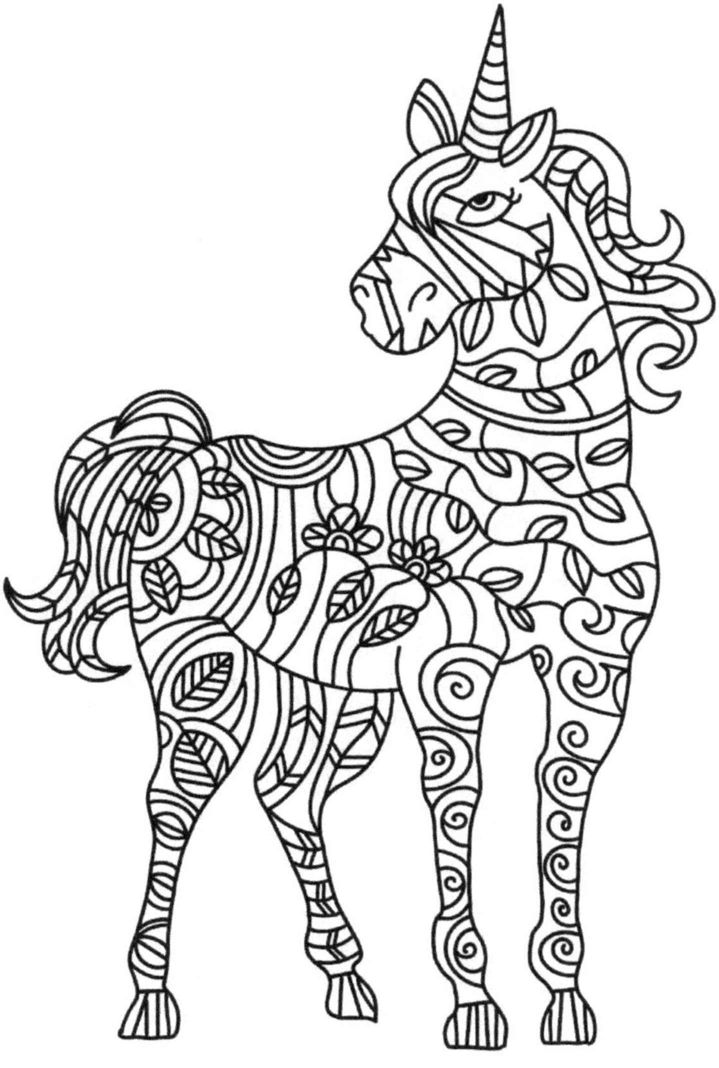

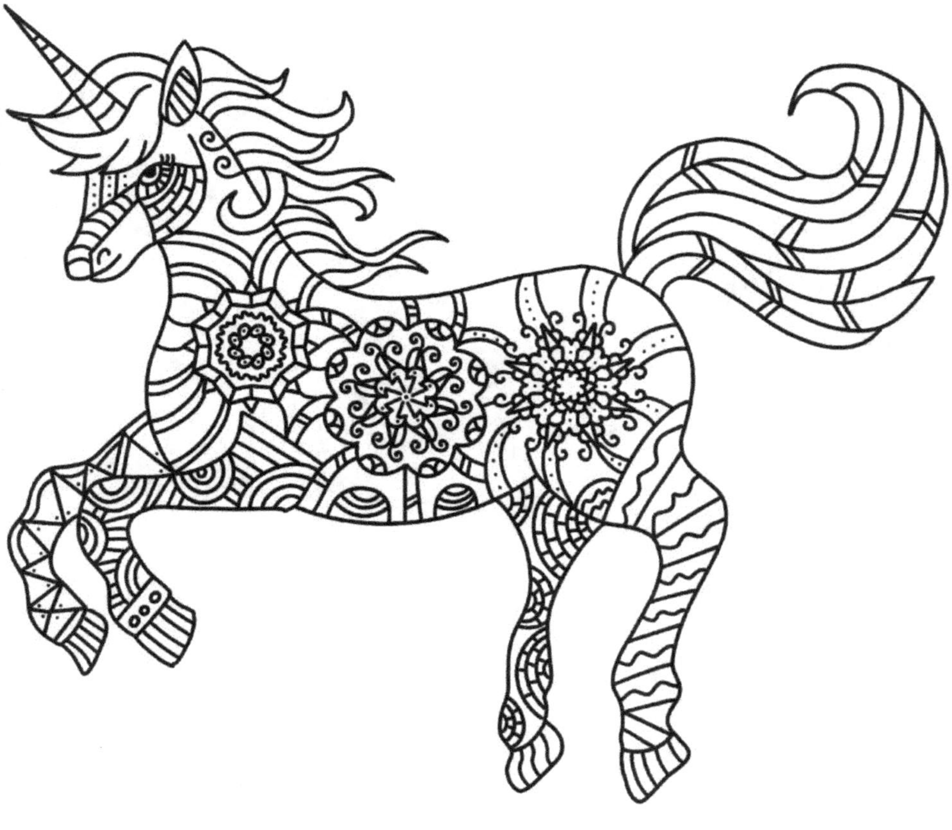

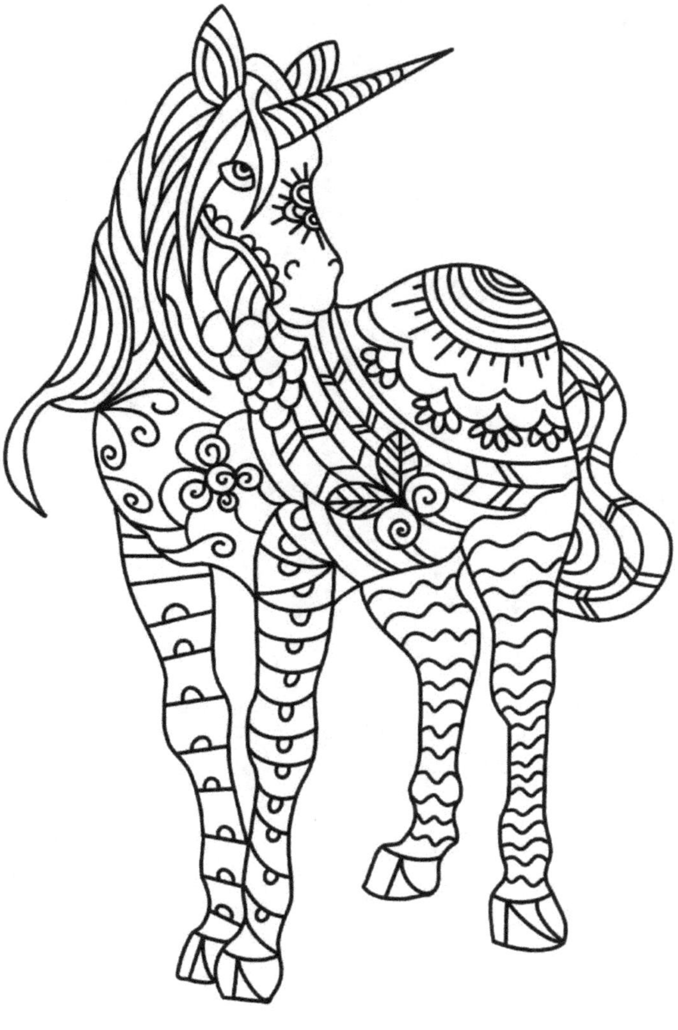

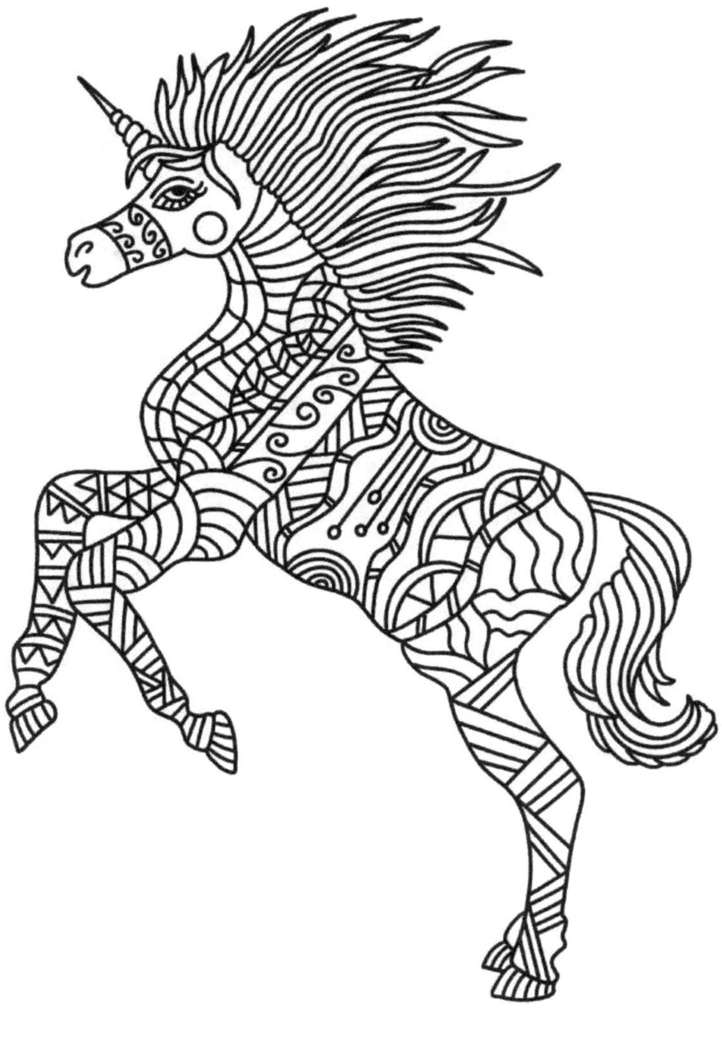

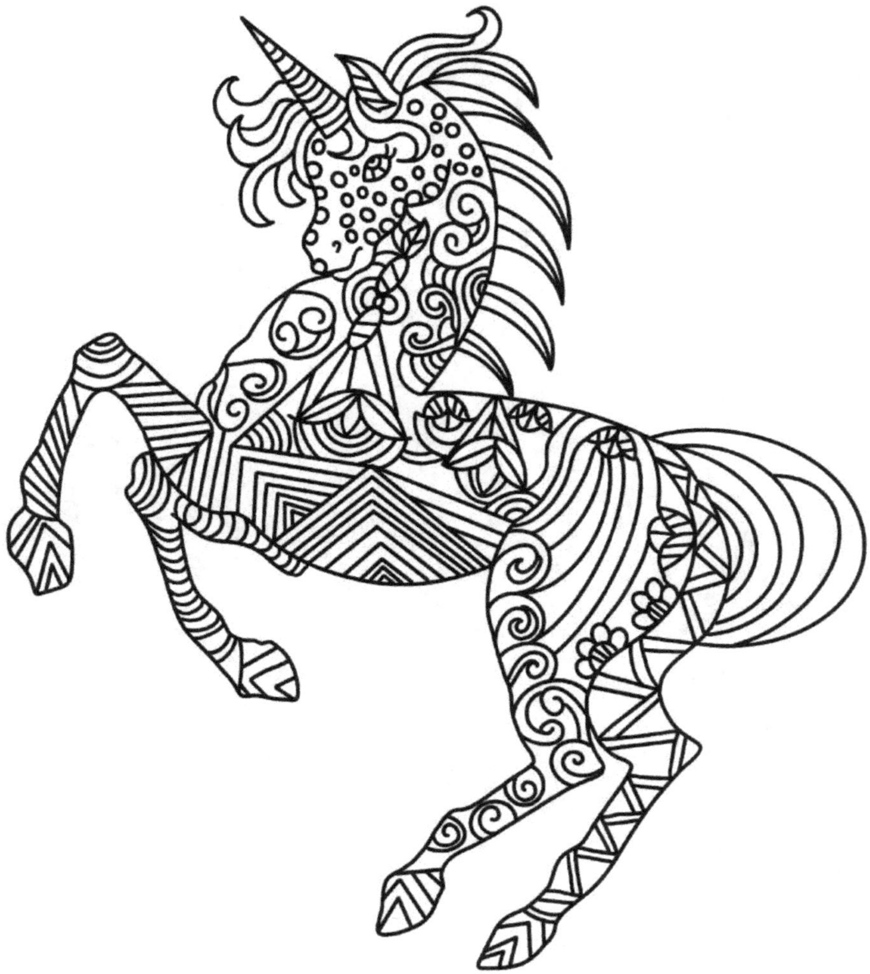

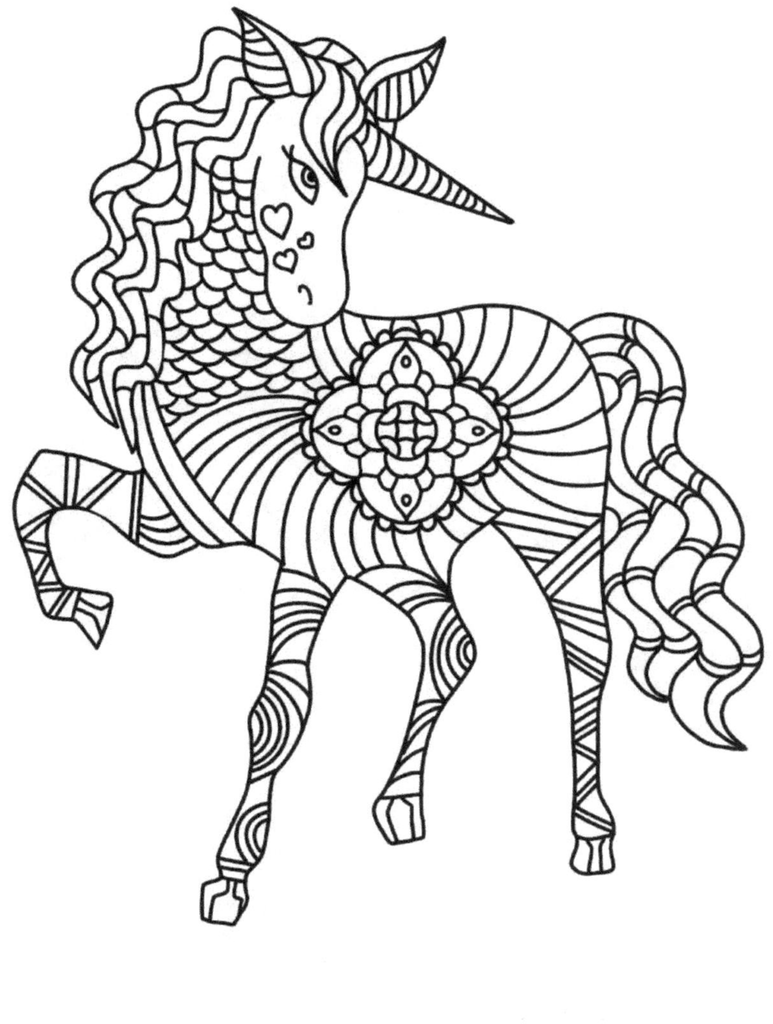

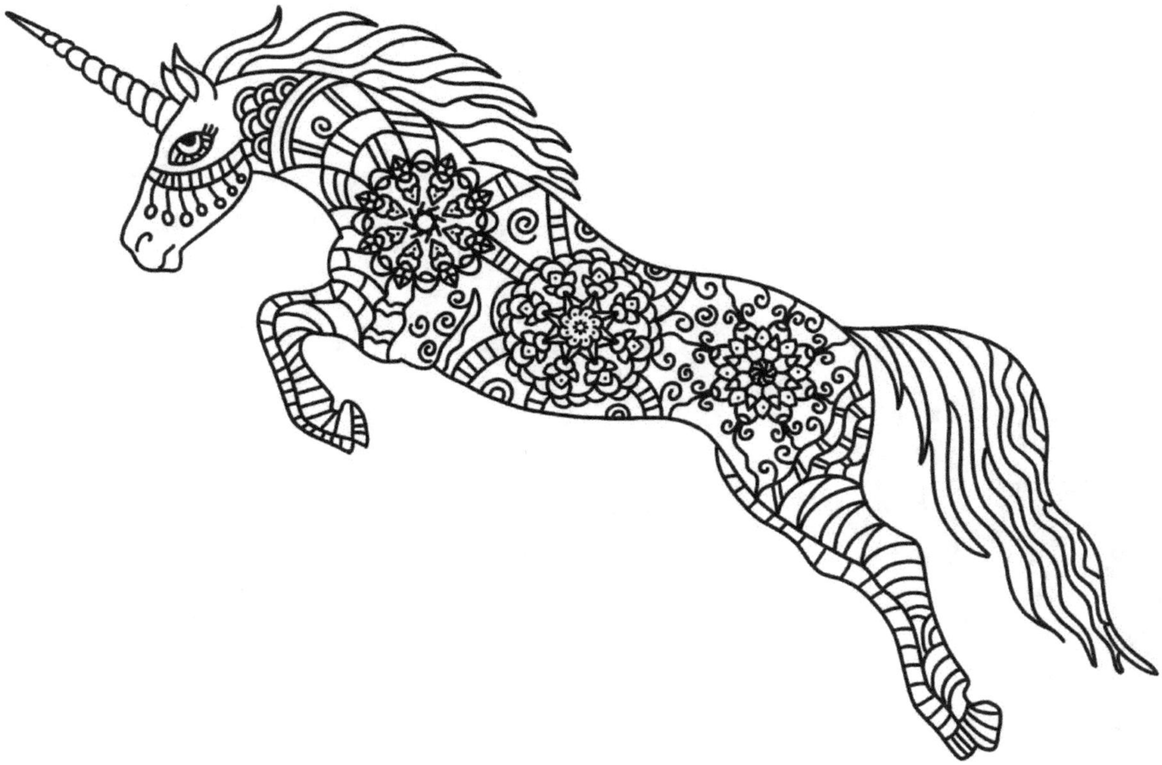

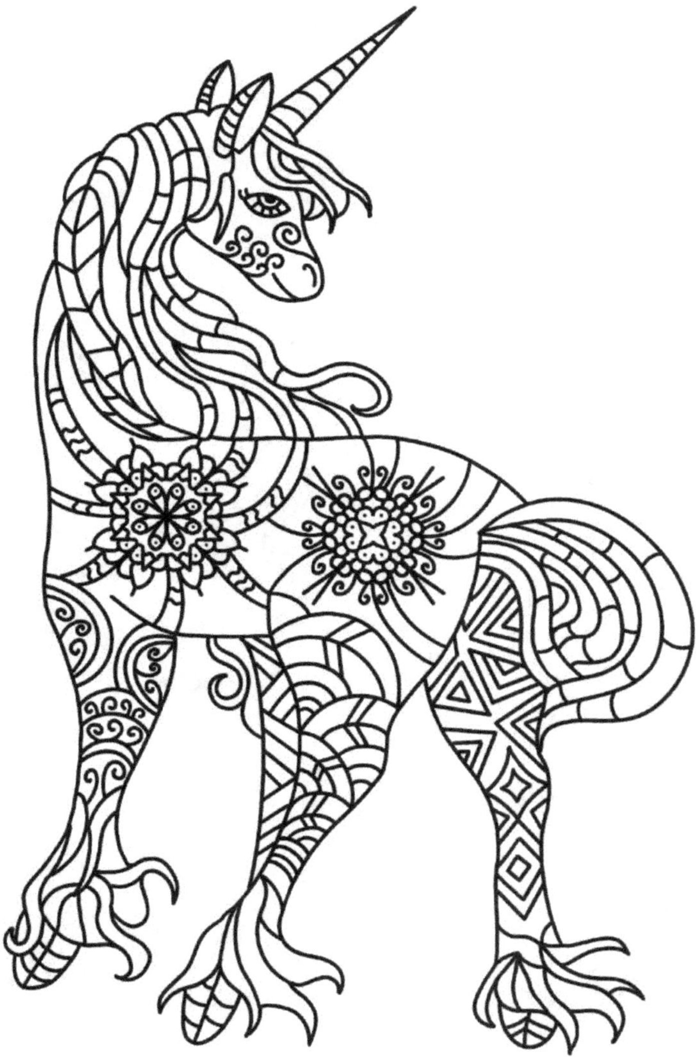

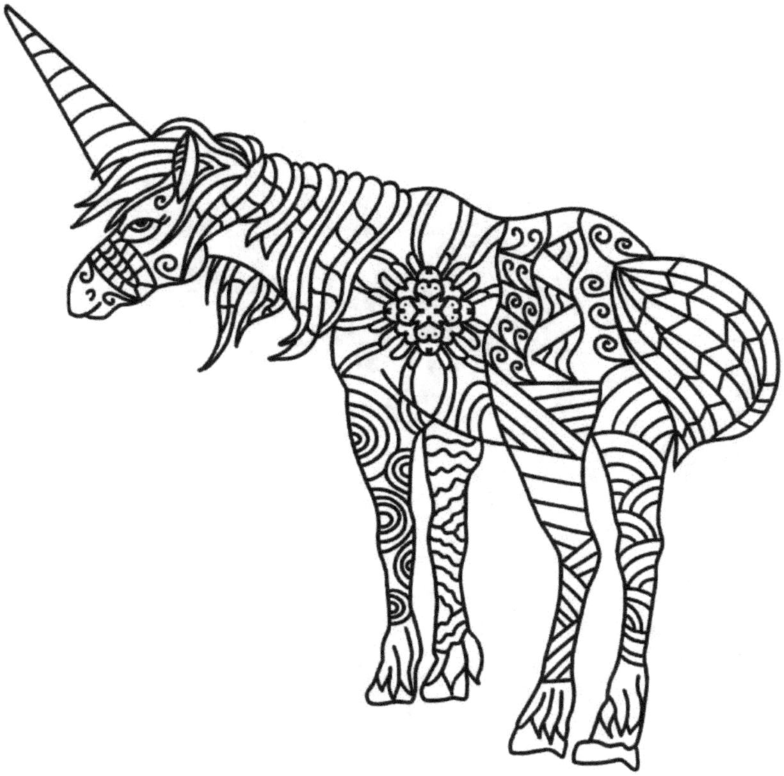

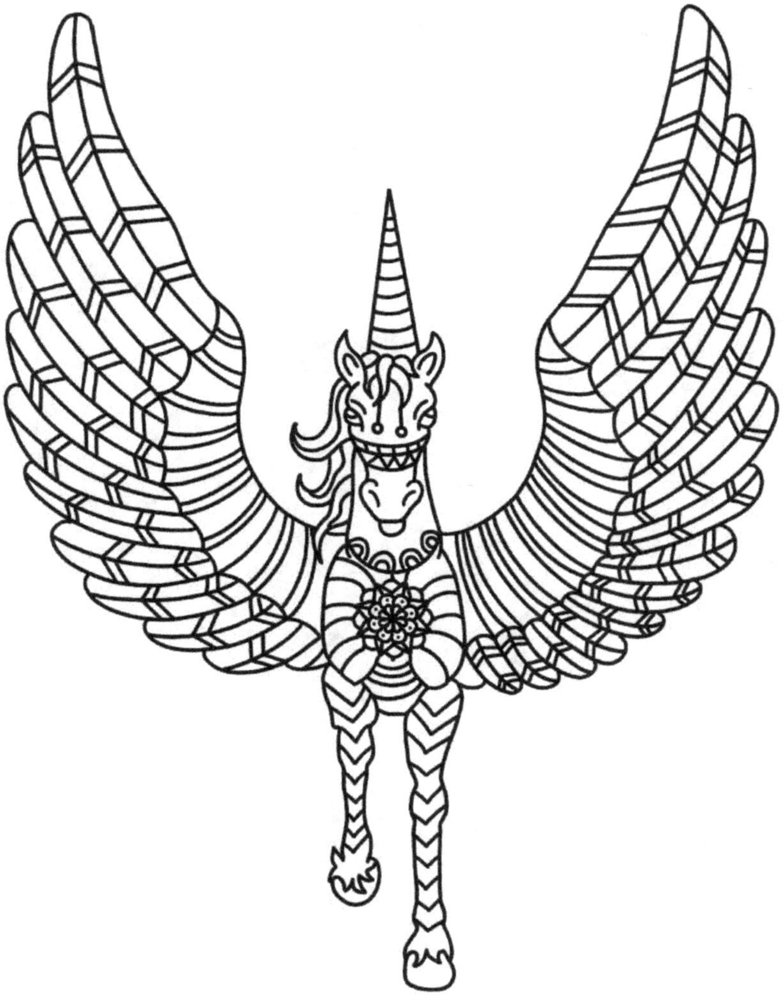

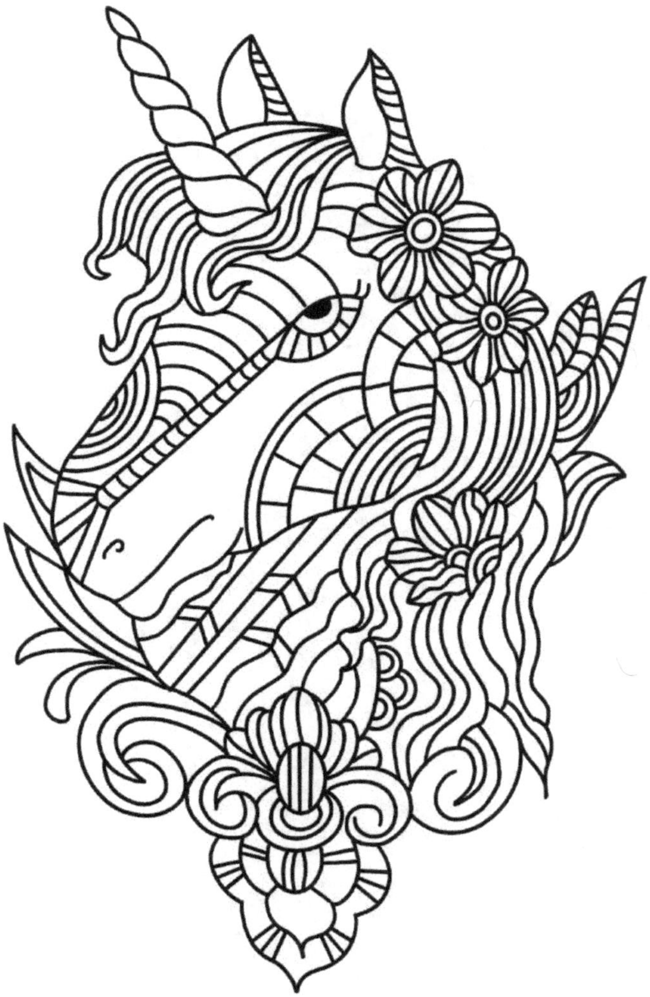

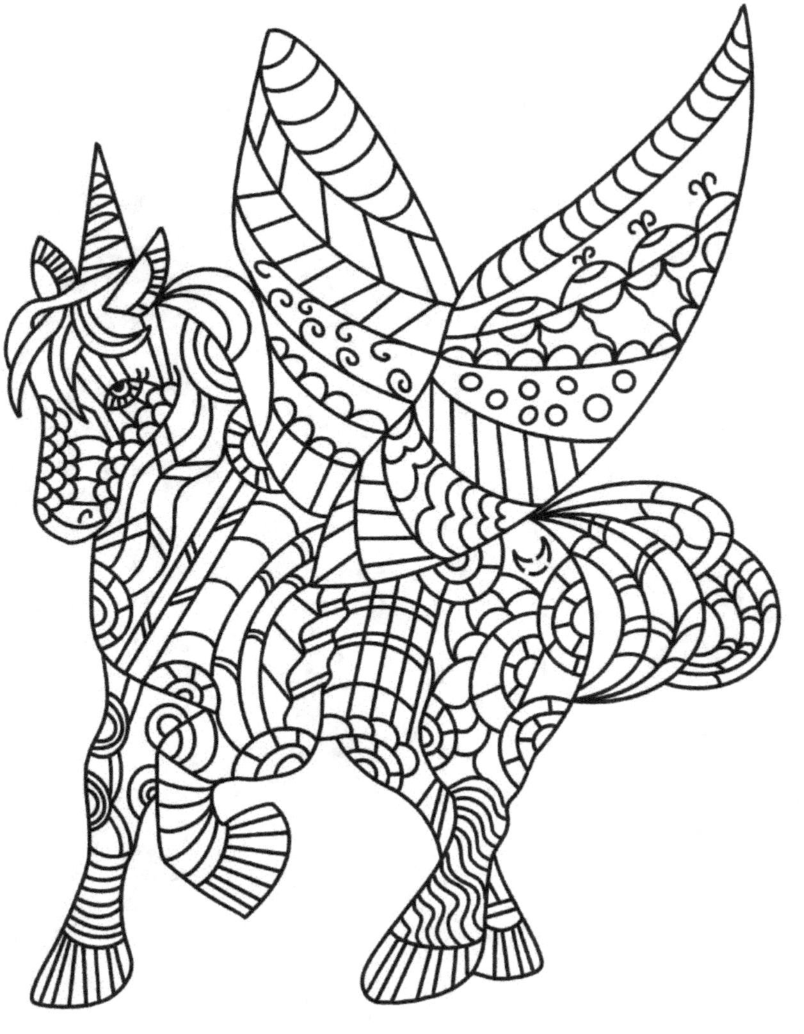

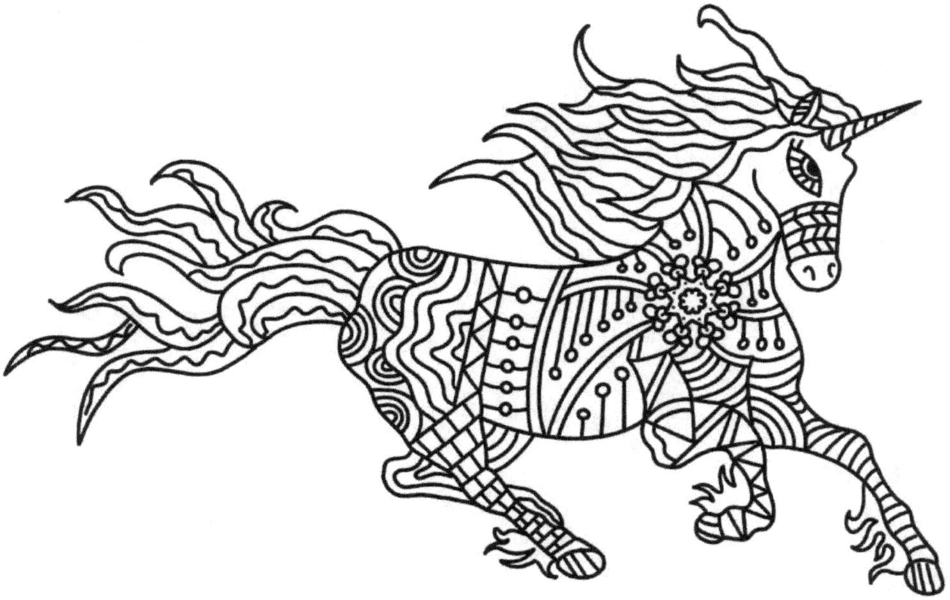

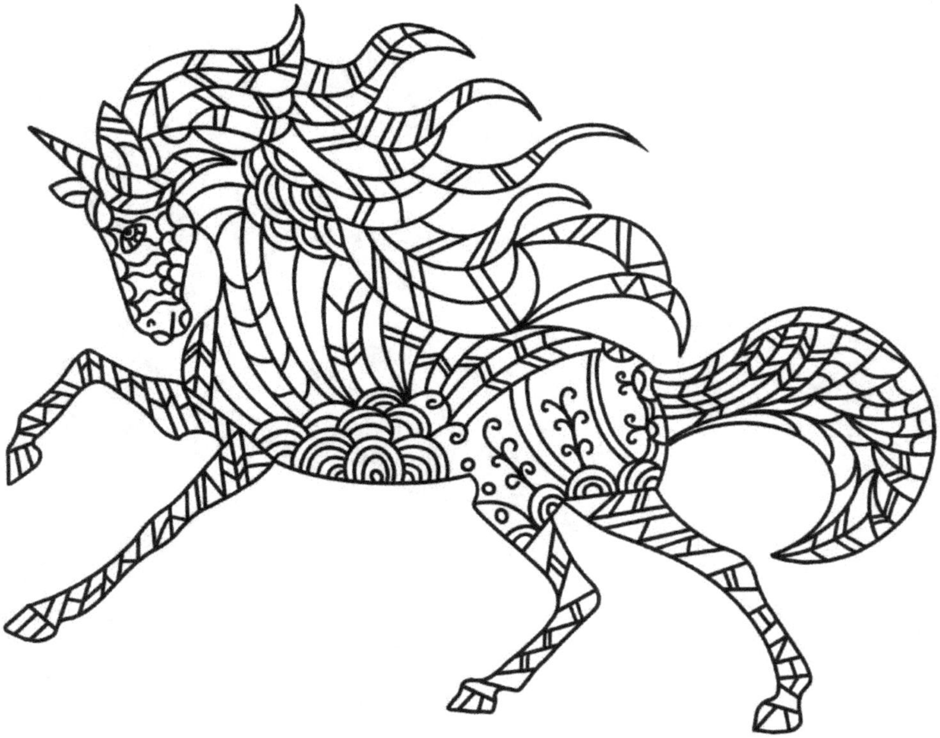

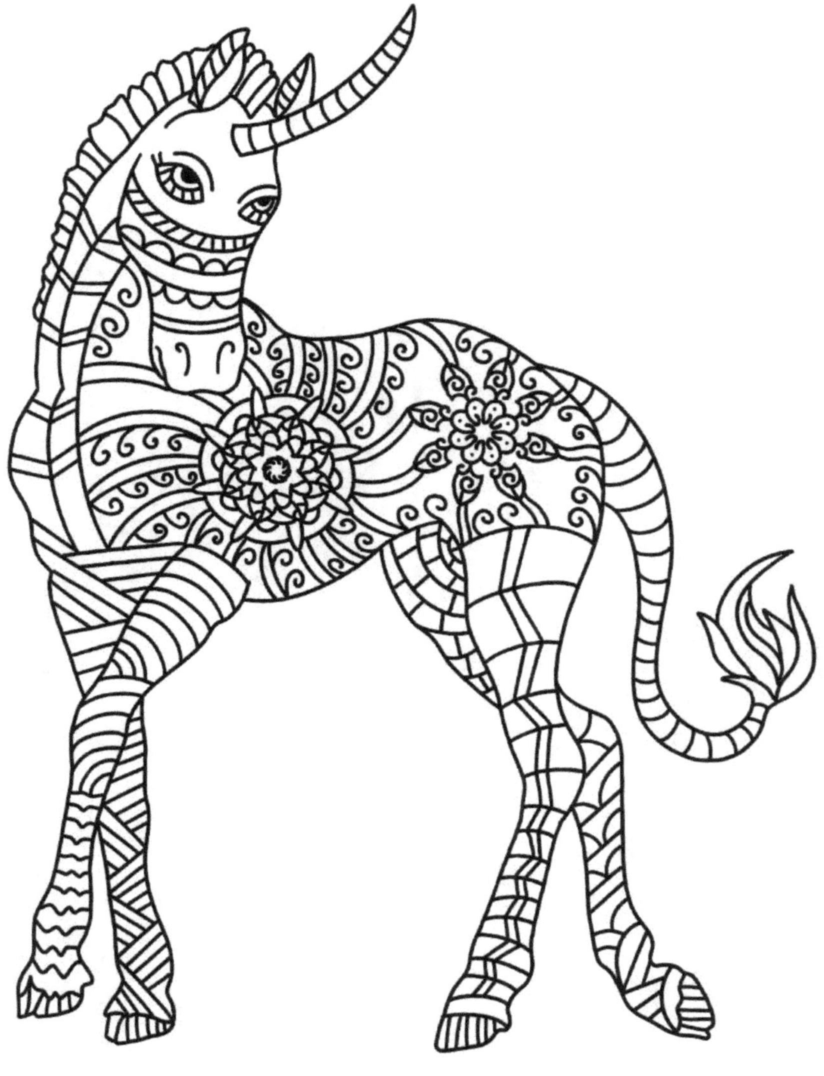

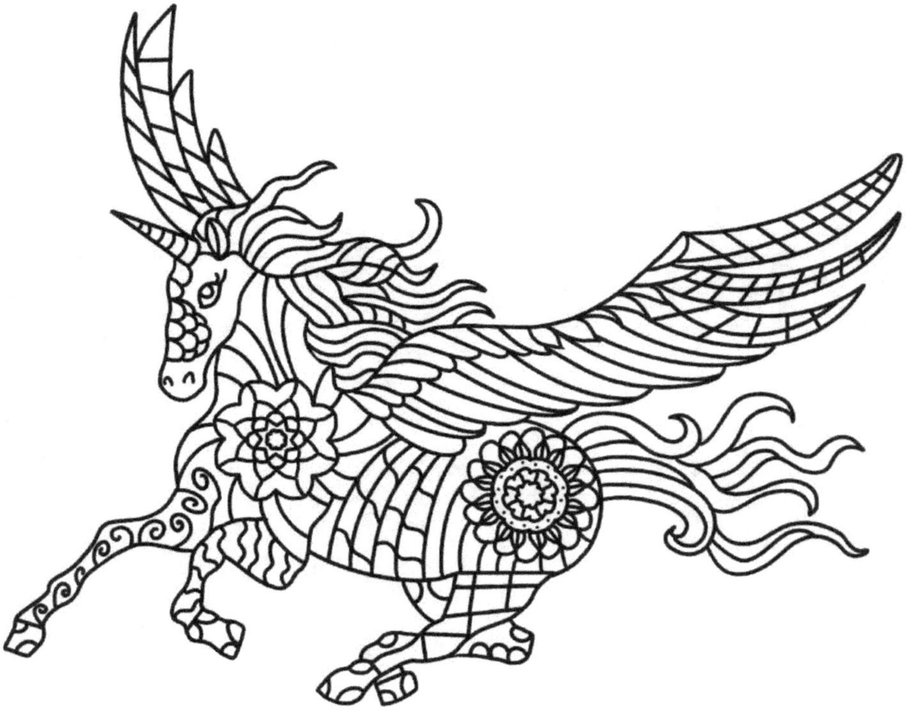

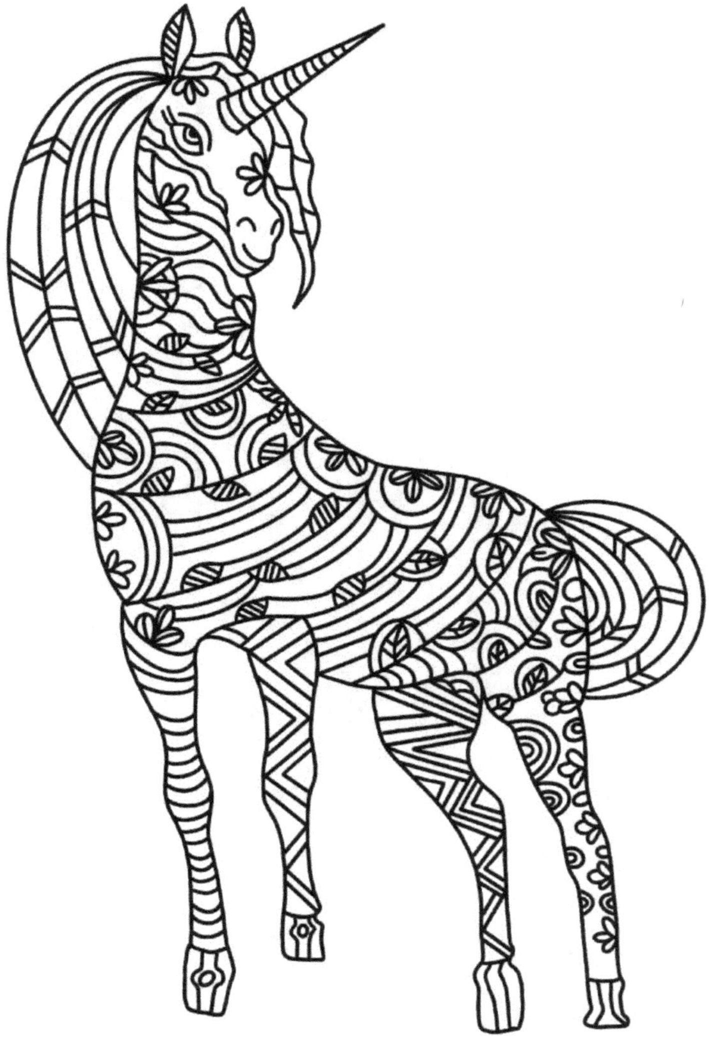

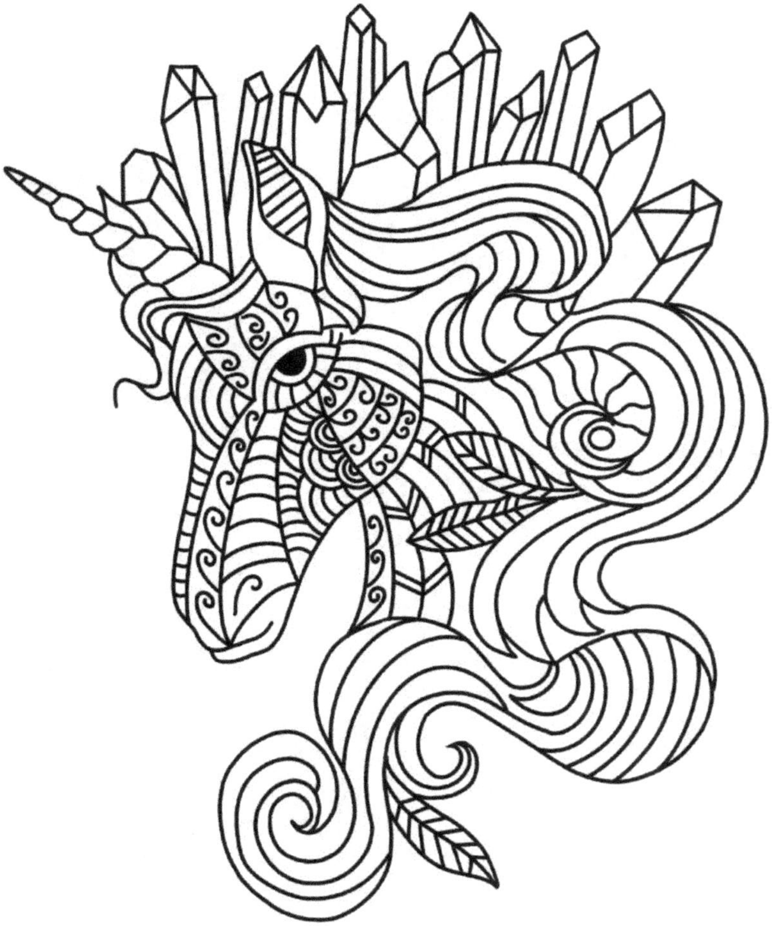

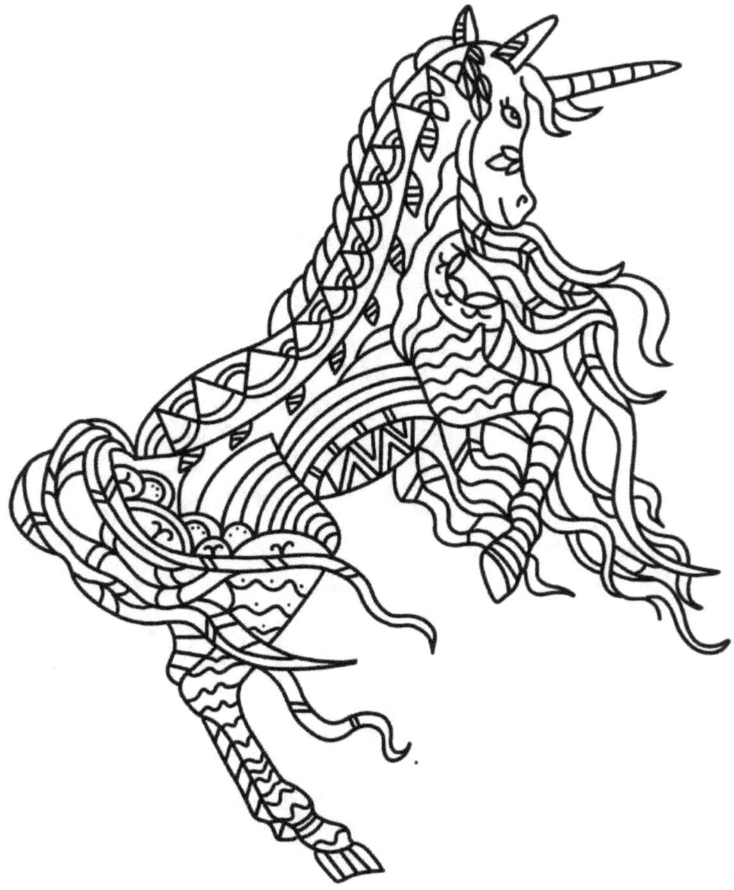

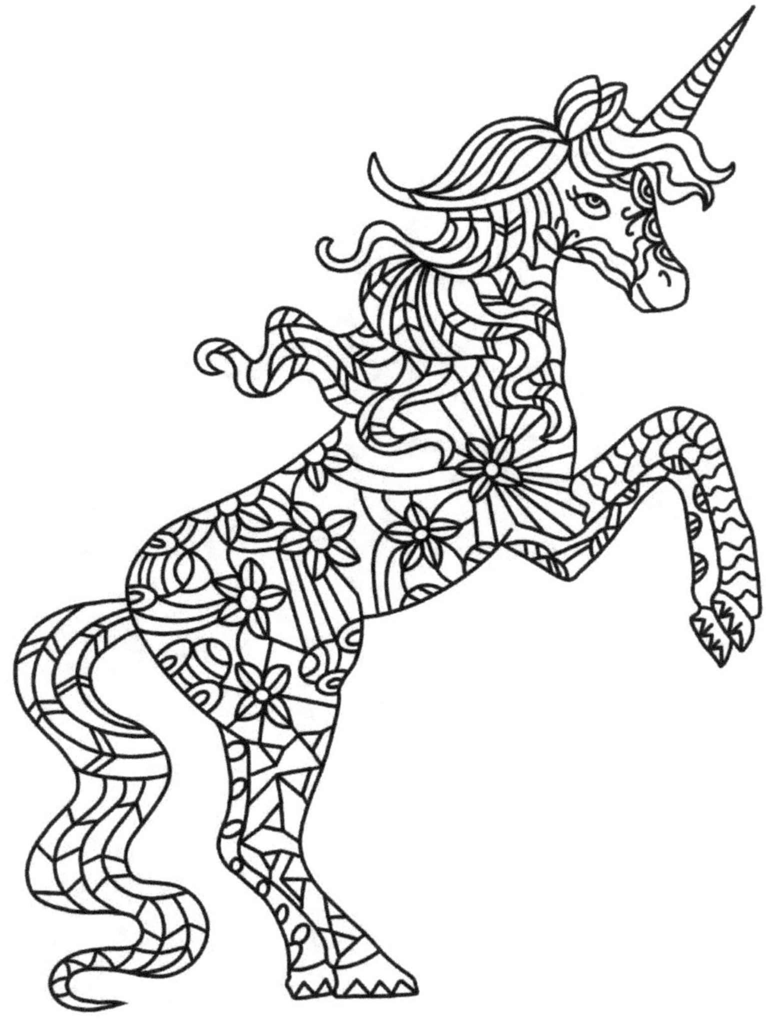

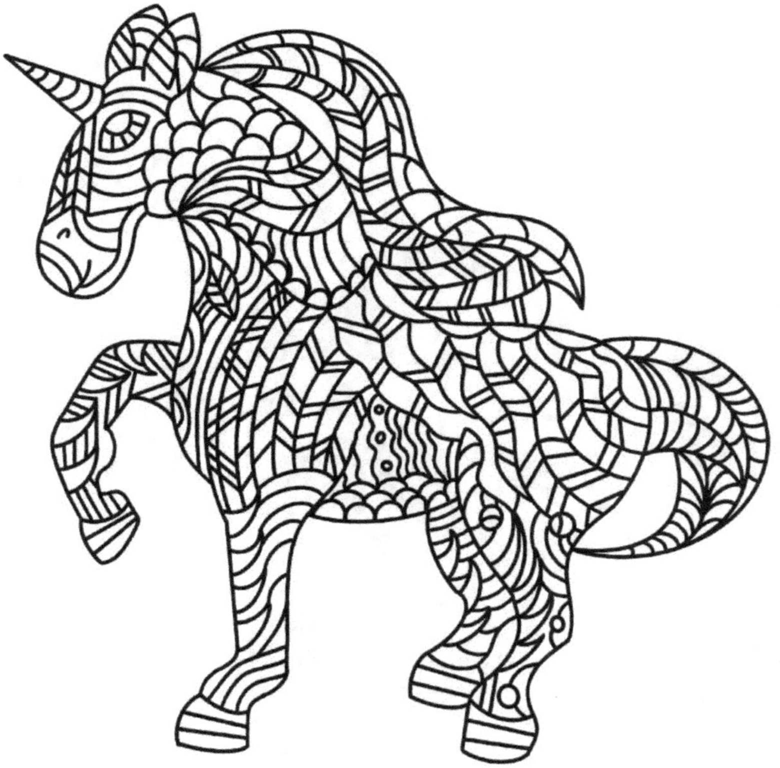

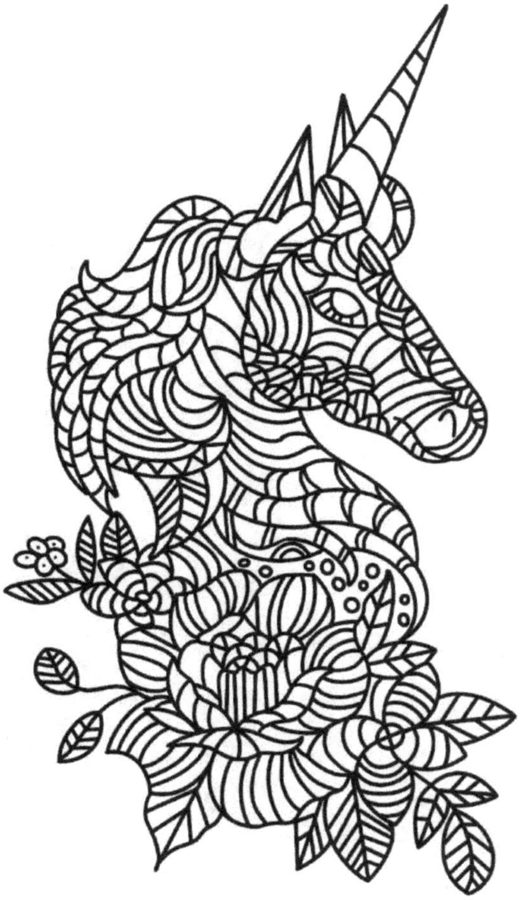

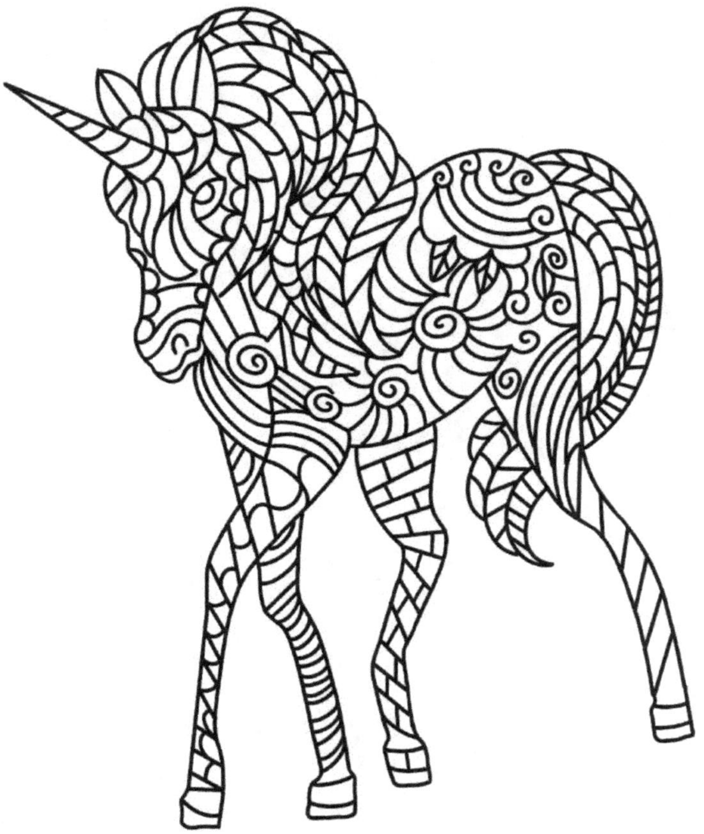

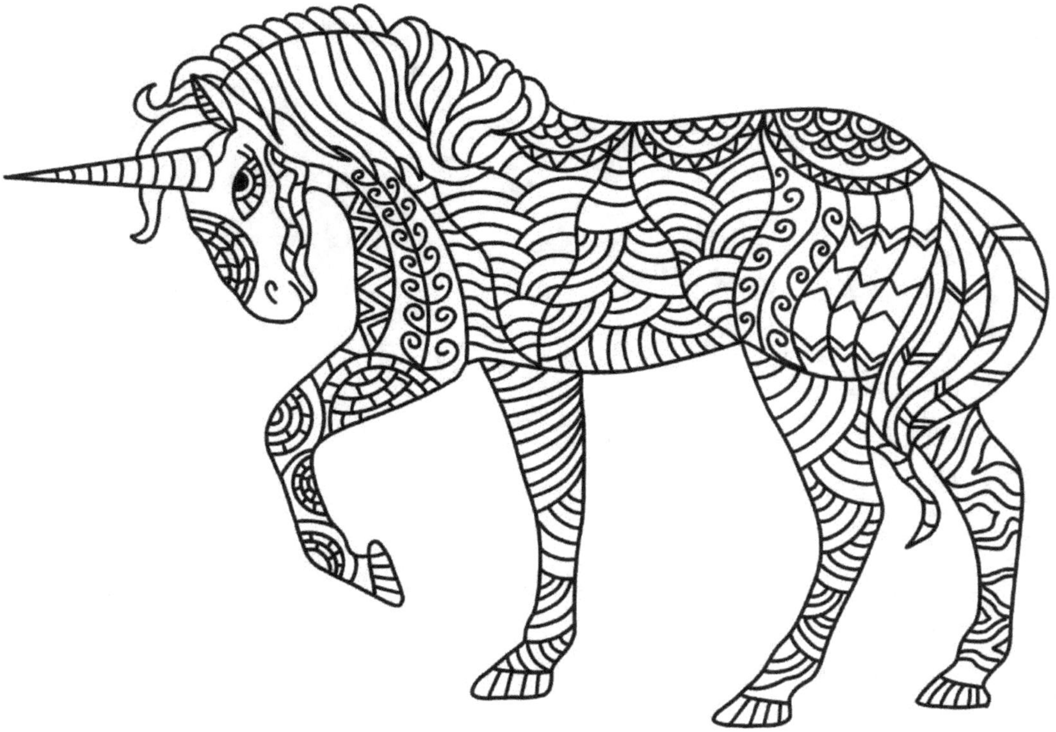

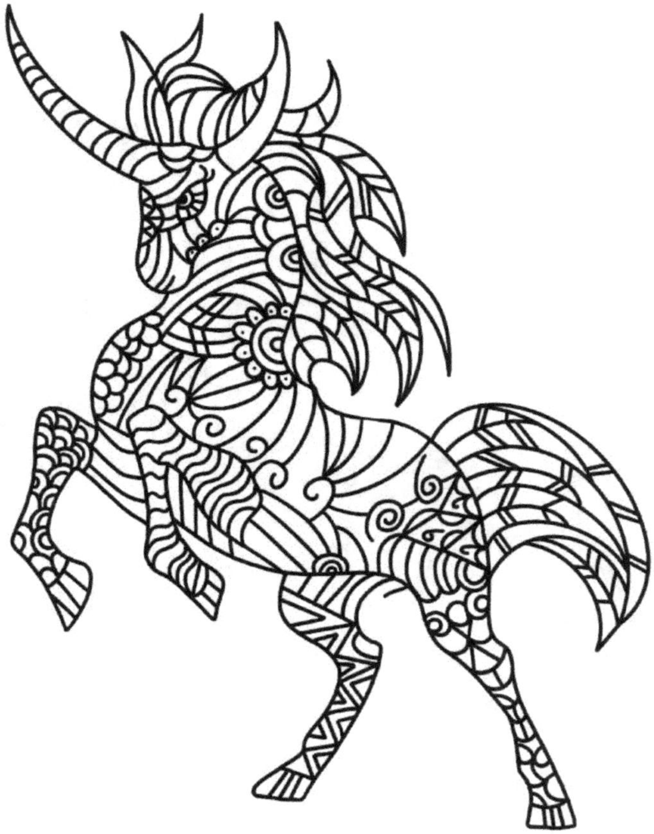

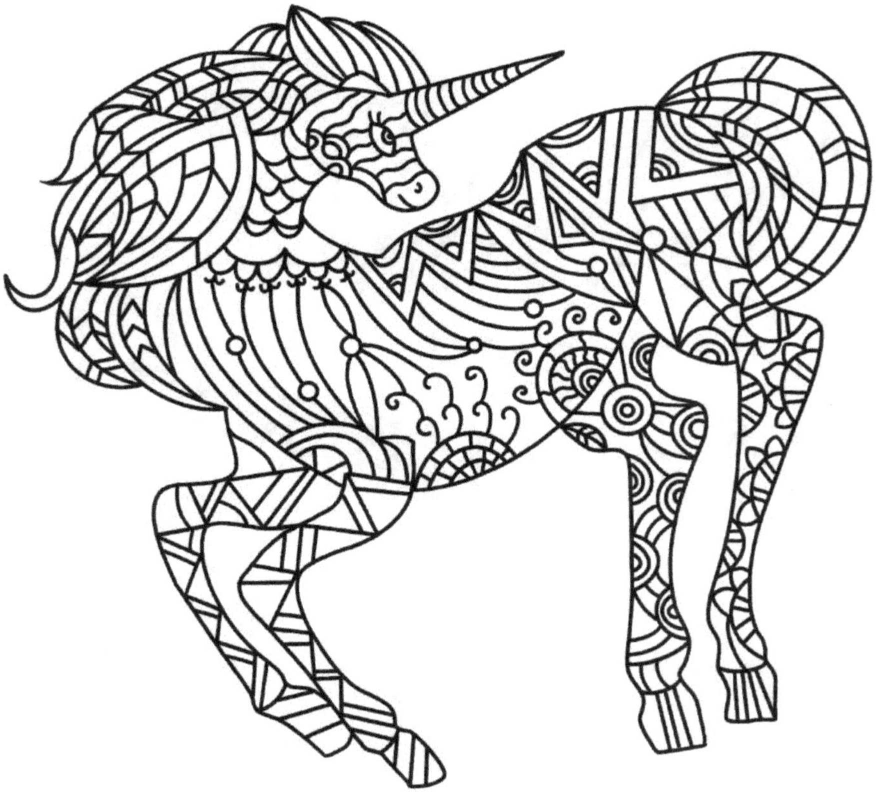

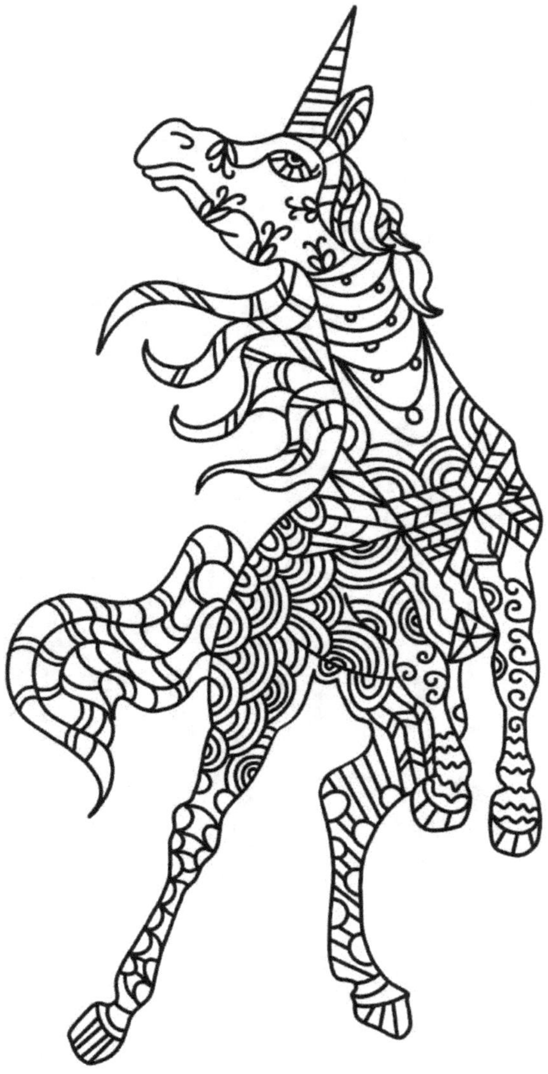

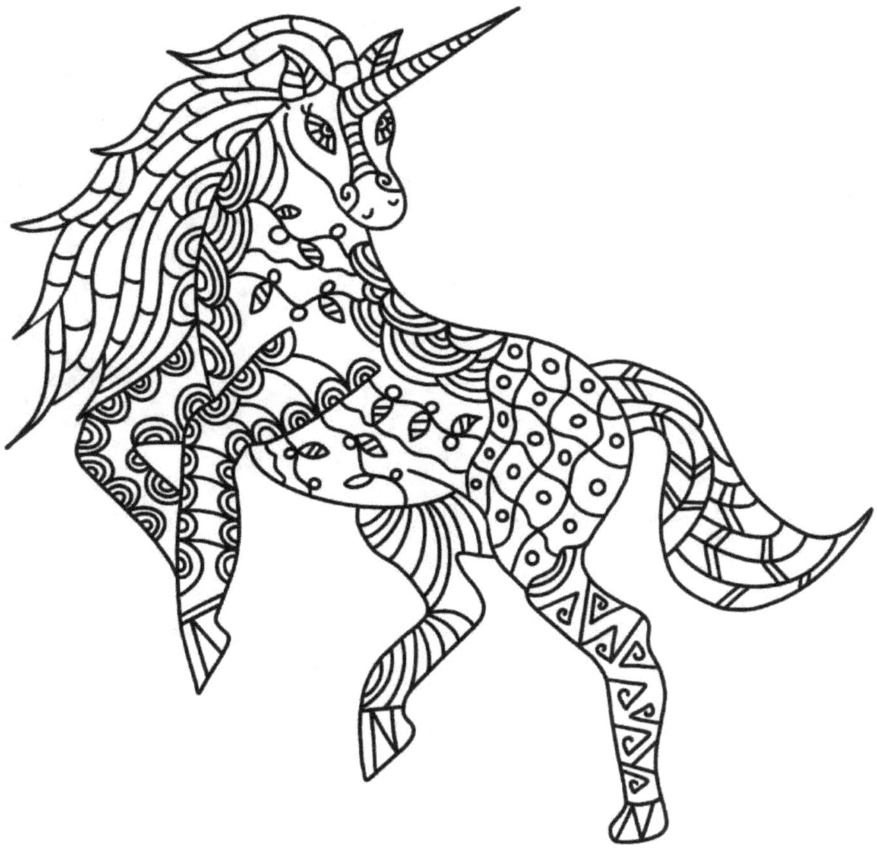

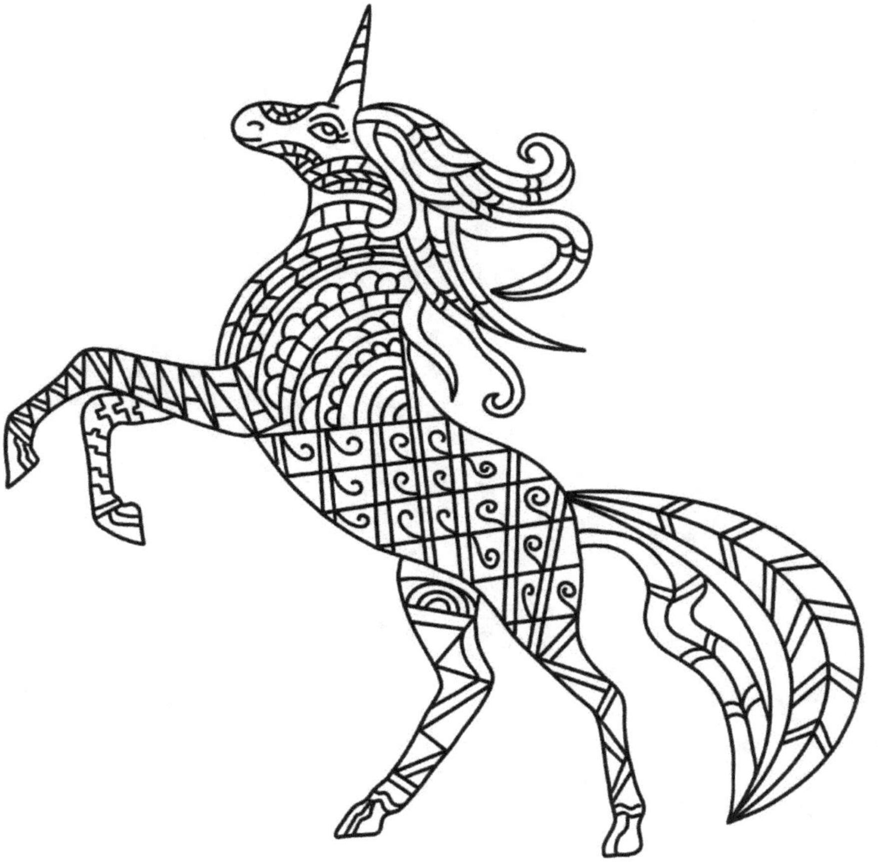

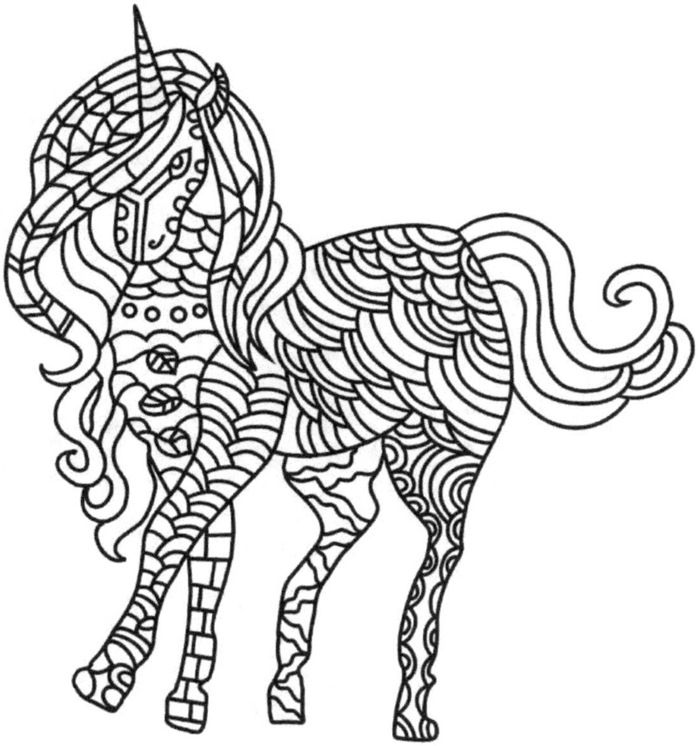

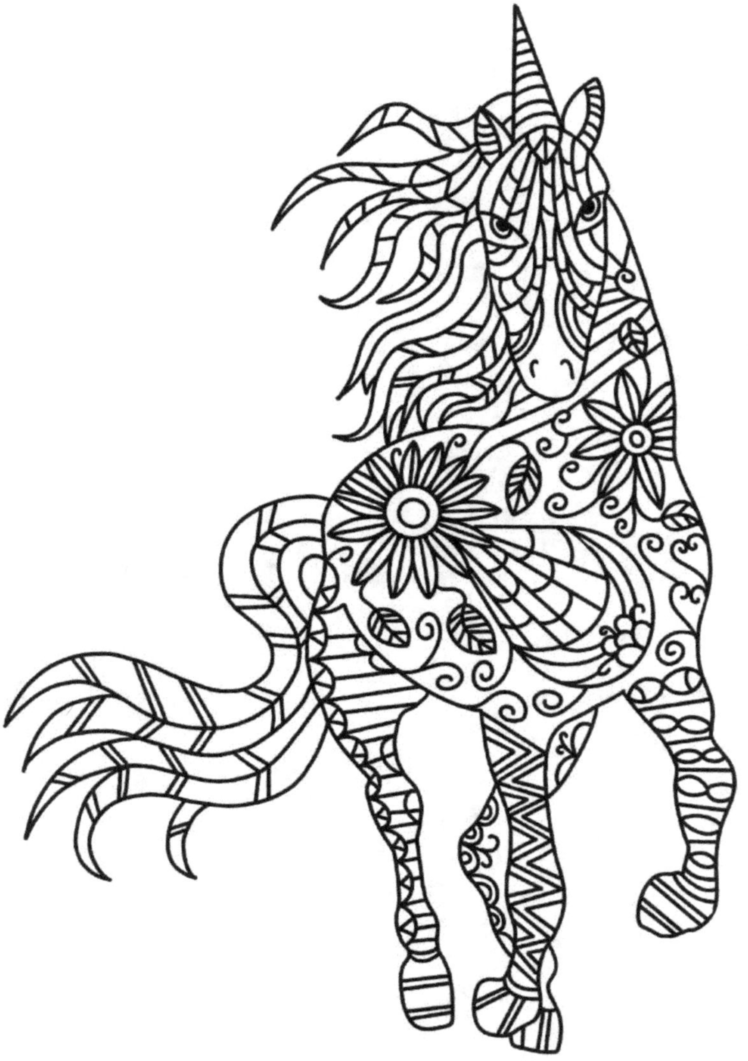

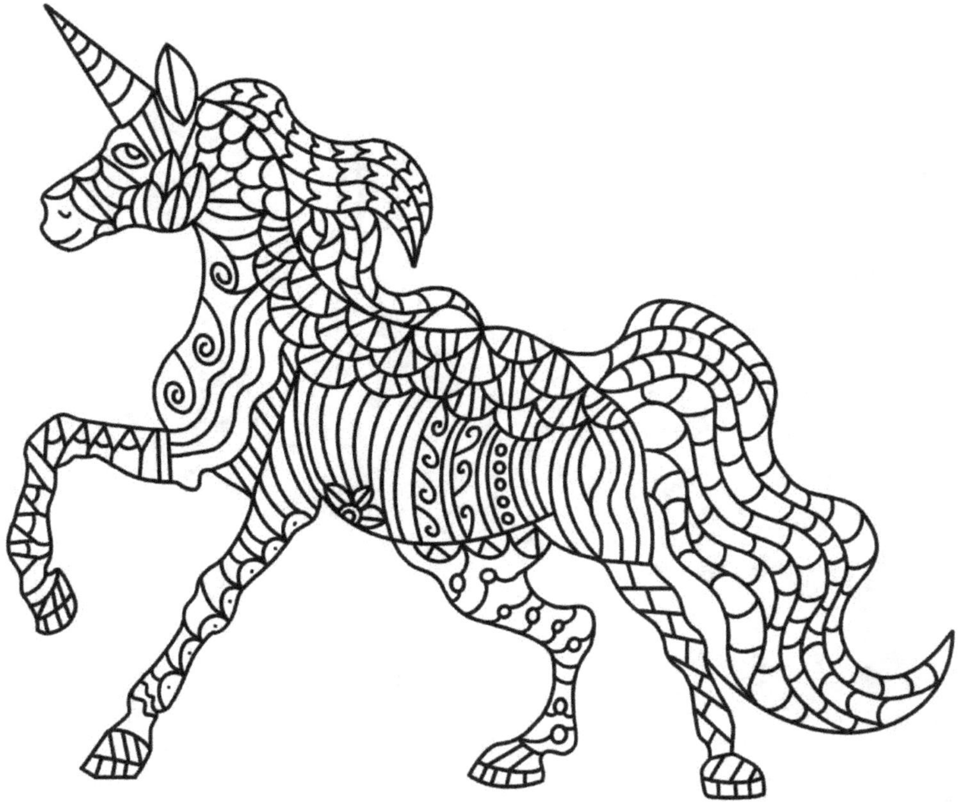

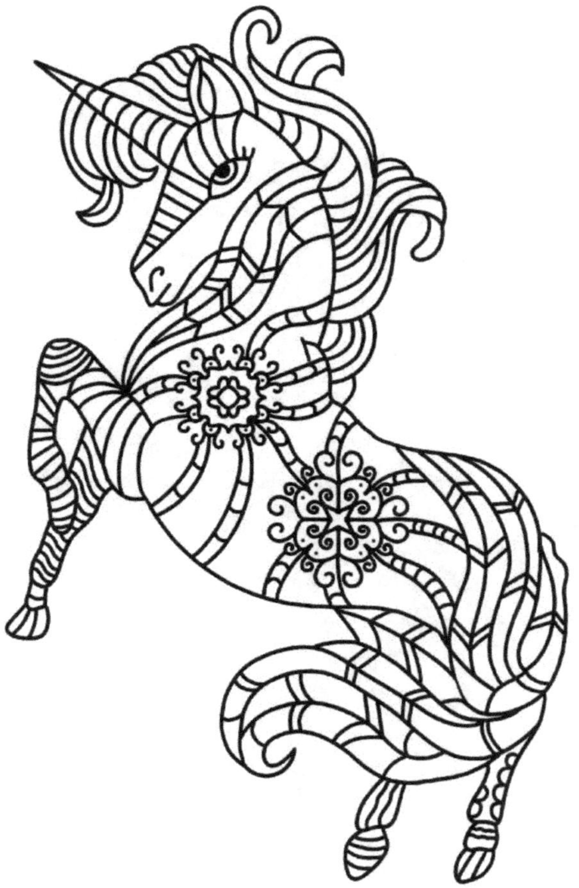

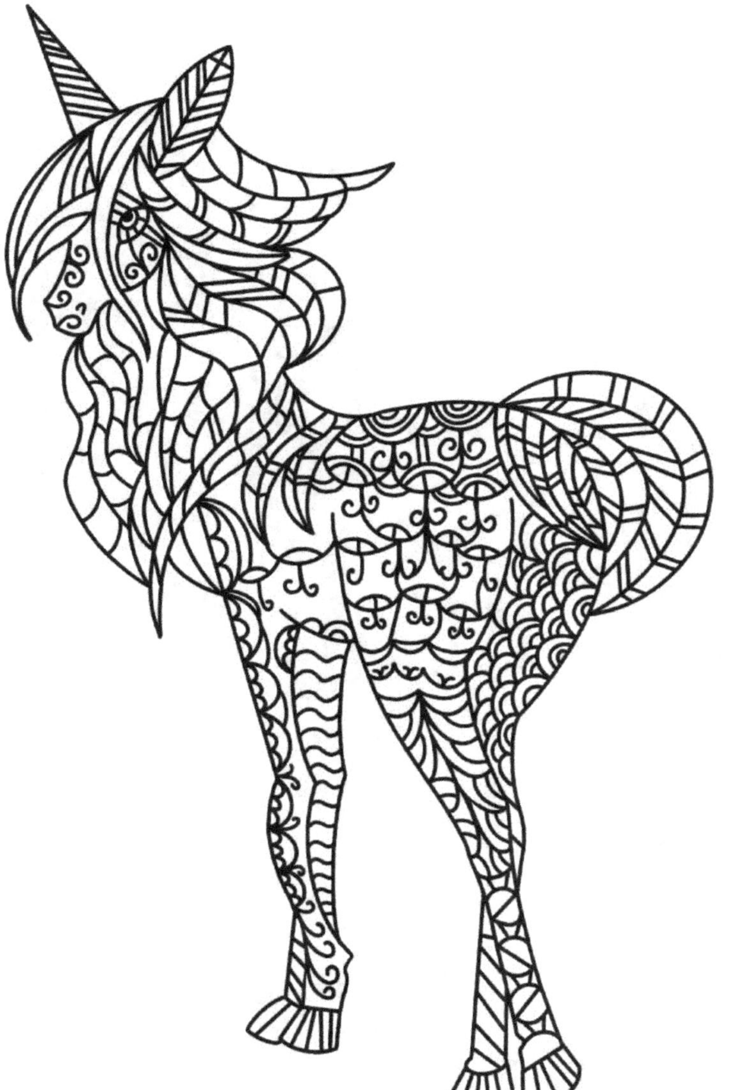

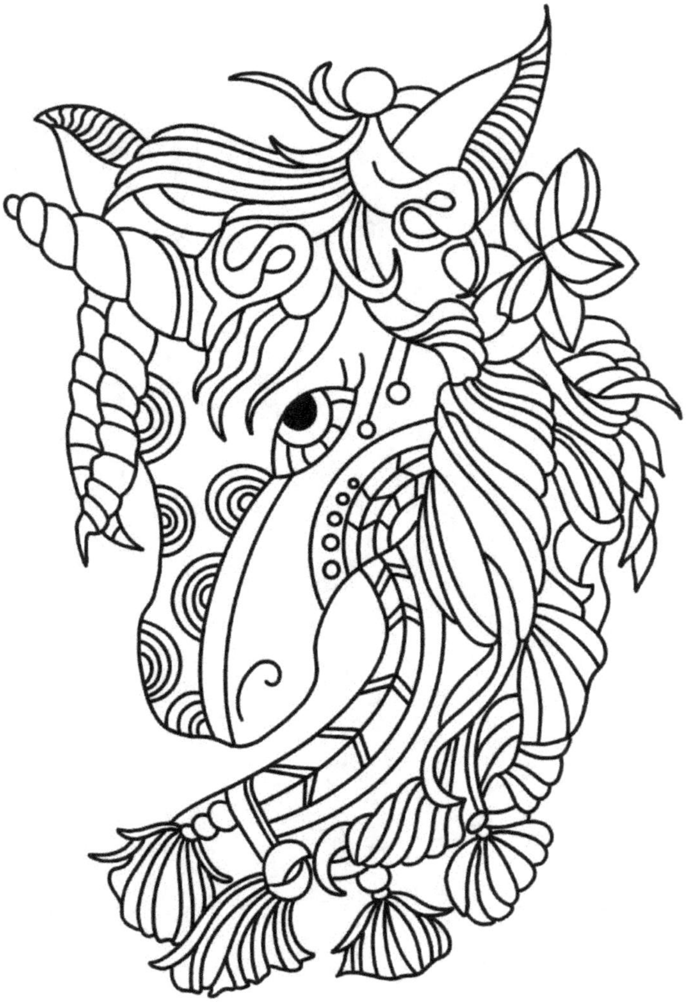

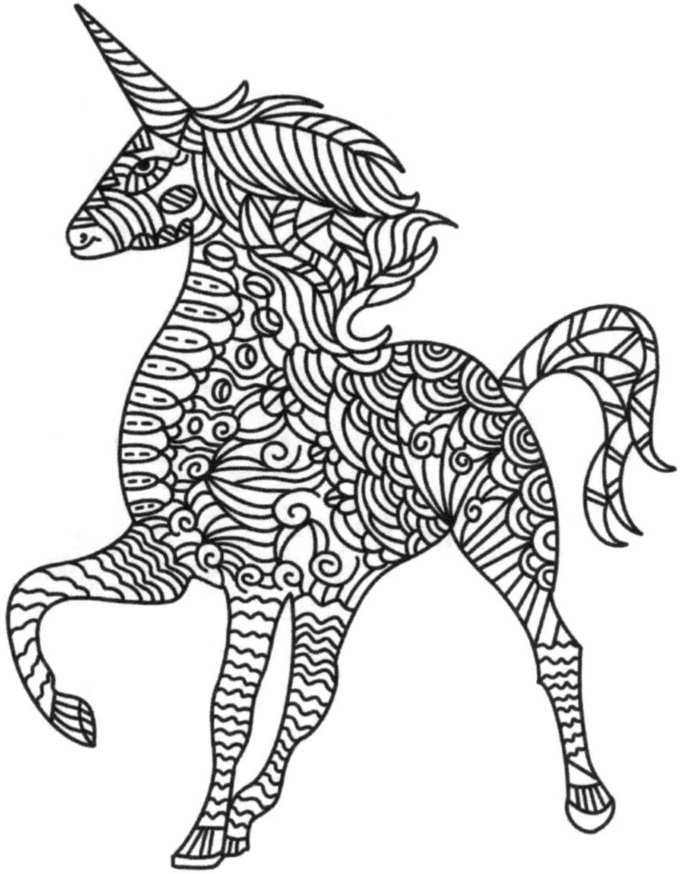

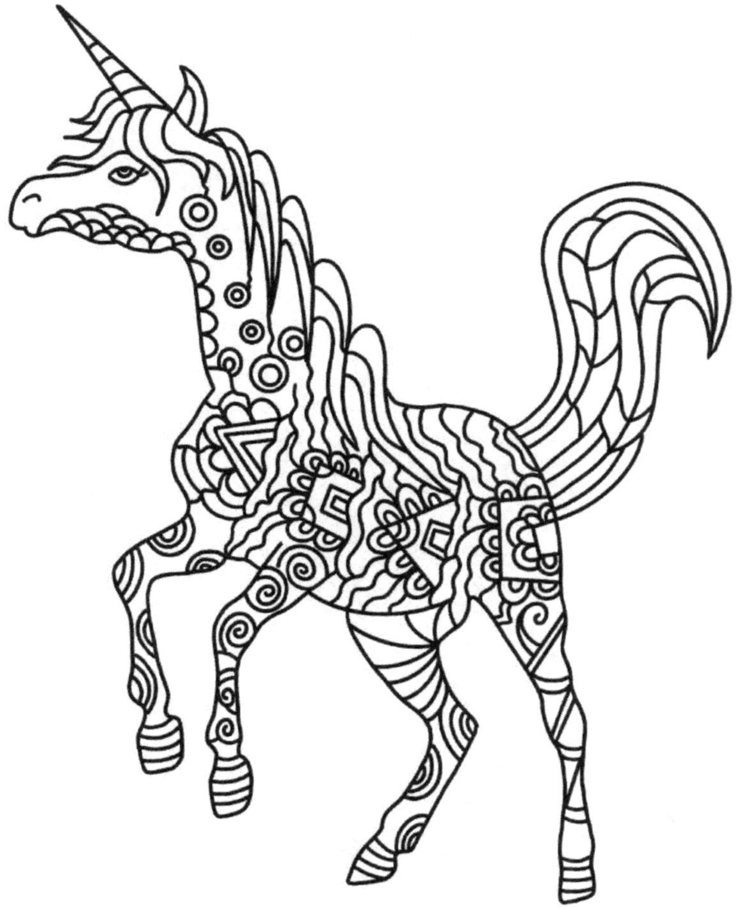

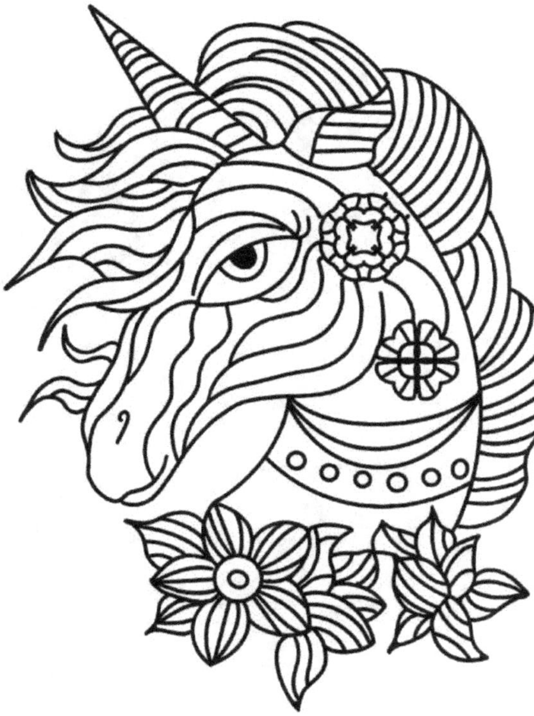

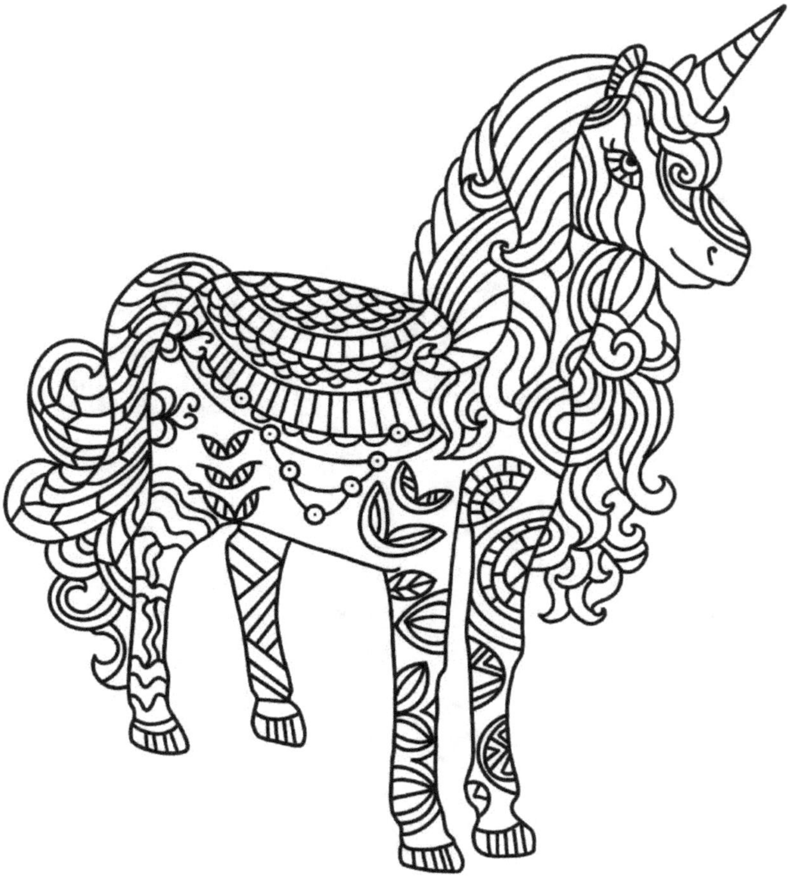

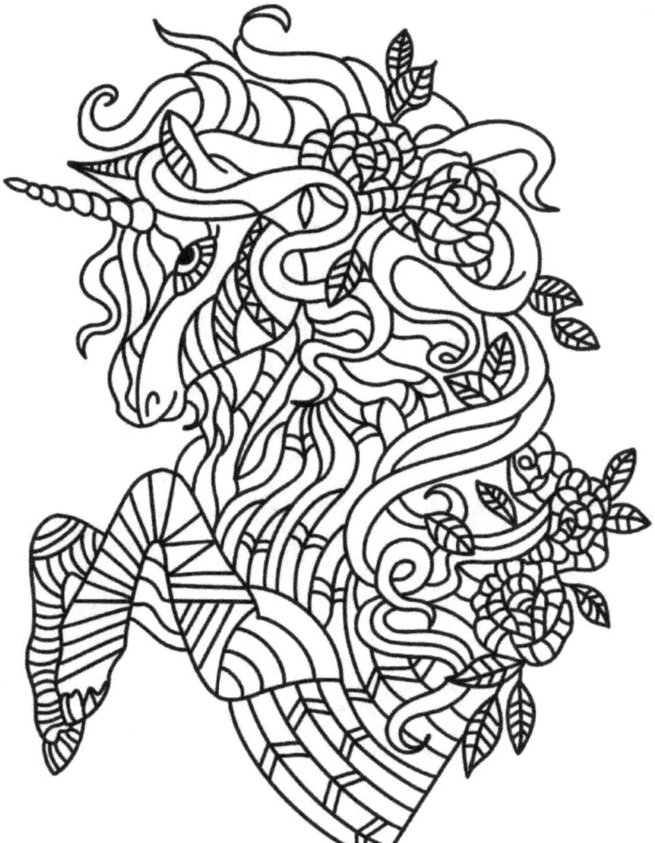

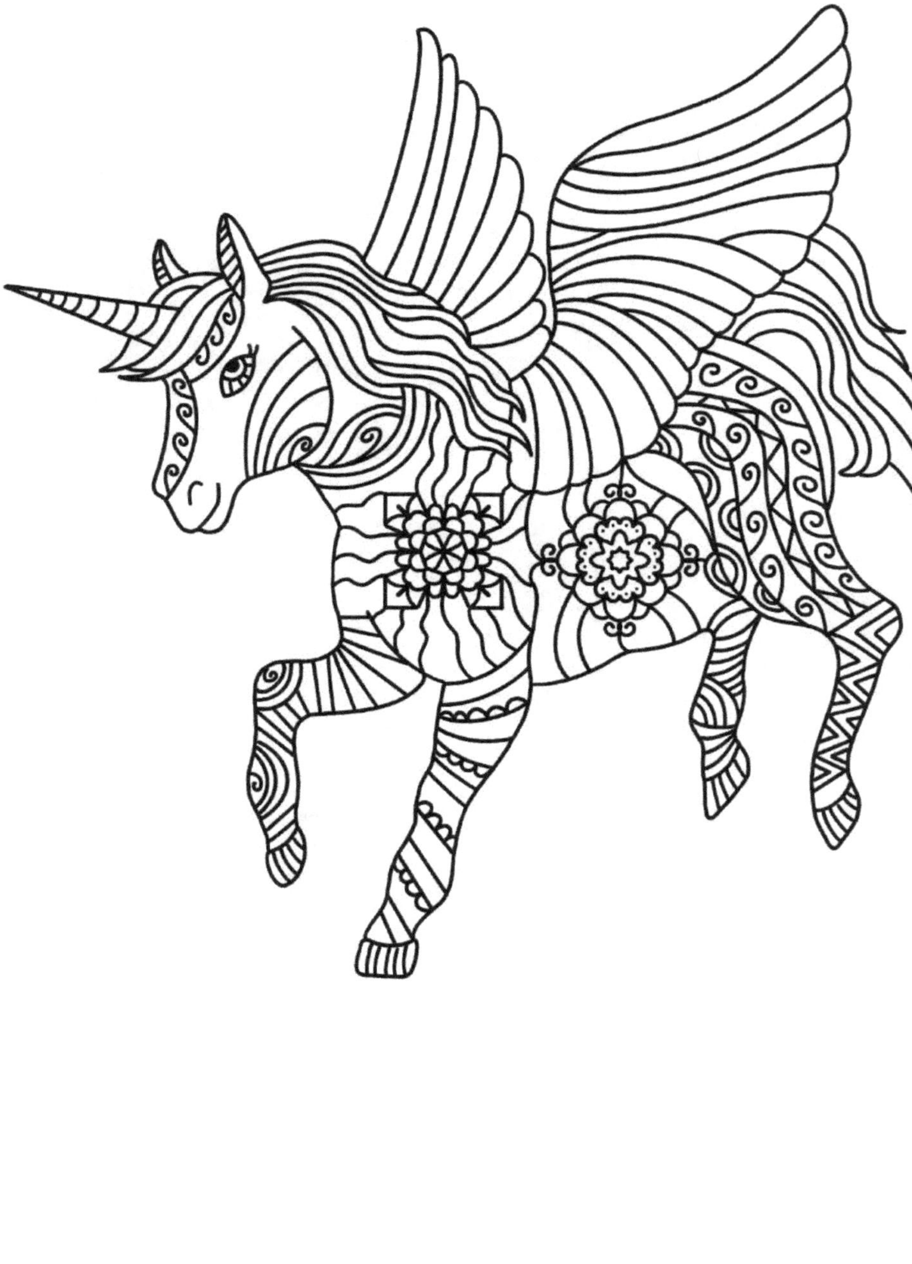

www.ingramcontent.com/pod-product-compliance
Lightning Source LLC
Chambersburg PA
CBHW080837220526
45467CB00008B/2309
* 9 7 8 1 7 1 0 1 6 1 2 7 4 *